Running an Indexing Business

Running an Indexing Business

EDITED BY JANET PERLMAN

AMERICAN SOCIETY OF INDEXERS

ISBN 1-57387-112-5

Copyright© 2001 by American Society of Indexers, Inc. and individual contributors as noted at each chapter.

All rights reserved. No part of this book may be reproduced in any form by any electronic or mechanical means, including information storage and retrieval systems, without the express written permission from the Society except by a reviewer who may quote brief passages for a review.

Published by
Information Today, Inc.
143 Old Marlton Pike
Medford, NJ 08055

in association with

The American Society of Indexers, Inc.
10200 West 44th Ave., Suite 304
Wheat Ridge, CO 80033

Printed in the United States of America

Publisher: Thomas H. Hogan, Sr.
Editor-in-Chief: John B. Bryans
Managing Editor: Deborah R. Poulson
Production Manager: M. Heide Dengler
Book Designer: Kara Mia Jalkowski

Table of Contents

Preface

Enid L. Zafran vii

Introduction

Janet Perlman ix

Contributors xi

Chapter 1:   The Business of Being in Business
L. Pilar Wyman 1

Chapter 2:   Managing Your Moonlighting Business
Carolyn G. Weaver 13

Chapter 3:   Report from the Front Lines
Dorothy DiRienzi 25

Chapter 4:   Independent Contractor Status: The Indexer's Role
Kate Mertes 31

Chapter 5:   Setting Fees
Jan C. Wright 37

Chapter 6:   Charging by the Entry
Nan Badgett 43

**Chapter 7: Educating Publishers
(or How to Deal with Low-Paying Clients)**
Maria Coughlin 45

Chapter 8: Office Space—Four Varieties
Margie Towery 47

Chapter 9: The ABCs of Project Management
Margie Towery 53

Chapter 10: Tips for a Winning Proposal
Janet Perlman 57

Chapter 11: Outsourcing the Outsourcing
Enid L. Zafran 67

Chapter 12: Late Payment Blues
Janet Perlman 71

Index
Janet Perlman 75

Preface

Janet Perlman graciously accepted the challenge of creating this book. Her hard work has paid off with a welcome addition to the literature that offers sound advice to freelance indexers on how to manage their businesses. This work picks up where *Starting an Indexing Business* leaves off. You now have established yourself as an indexer and are getting jobs, but you have not resolved the complex issues of taxes, writing proposals, setting fees for various types of work, and deciding whether to use others to help on projects. The articles in this volume will help you understand more fully the pros and cons before you take action and discuss real-world experiences of successful indexers who have dealt with the same situations that you now face.

On behalf of the American Society of Indexers (ASI), I would like to acknowledge all the authors: Nan Badgett, Joanne Clendenen, Maria Coughlin, Dorothy DiRienzi, Kate Mertes, Alexandra Nickerson, Marilyn Rowland, Sandi Schroeder, Richard Shrout, Barbara Stroup, Margie Towery, Carolyn Weaver, Jan Wright, Pilar Wyman, and Enid Zafran. Janet has served in several capacities on the project and deserves recognition as an author, the editor, and the indexer.

We are also grateful for the assistance of ITI's staff—in particular, John Bryans, Deborah Poulson, and Heather Rudolph. Their expertise in publishing enhances ASI's ability to meet its educational goals for the indexing profession.

For additional information about ASI, contact:

> American Society of Indexers
> 10200 West 44th Avenue, Suite 304
> Wheat Ridge, CO 80033
> Phone: (303) 463-2887
> Fax: (303) 422-8894
> Email: info@asindexing.org

For a list of ASI publications or to order ASI books, contact Information Today, Inc., ASI's official publisher:

> Information Today, Inc.
> 143 Old Marlton Pike
> Medford, NJ 08055
> Phone: 1-800-300-9868 (or 609-654-6266)
> Fax: 609-654-4309
> E-mail: custserv@infotoday.com
> http://www.infotoday.com/catalog/books.htm#asi

Enid L. Zafran
Publications Committee Chair

Introduction

So often we speak of "the art and science" of indexing. For those of us who are self-employed, there is a third side—the business side. Freelancers, whether full-time or running their indexing business "on the side," must be concerned with issues that indexers as employees don't have to think about.

We are, after all, small-business owners. As such, not only must we be concerned with the techniques of producing our product, the index, and with its quality—we must also be concerned with setting rates, office space, ergonomics, bookkeeping and taxes, independent contractor status, copyright, the possibility of using subcontractors, writing proposals, and anything else that comes under the umbrella of running a business.

After a long time as a part-time indexer, I made the transition from moonlighting to full-time indexer a little more than 10 years ago. I am pleased to say that, with a lot of hard work, I am financially successful. My business is quite profitable, and I earn a good living. I attribute this to the fact that I have always viewed my indexing as a business and have tried to run my indexing practice in the most businesslike manner. I have tried to make financial decisions and decisions about how to spend my time in terms of what is best to grow my business.

For those who are just starting out, the best source of information is the companion book to this one—*Starting an Indexing Business*, Third Edition (1998, American Society of Indexers, Enid Zafran, editor), available from Information Today, Inc. This book, *Running an Indexing Business*, assumes that you have taken those initial steps of starting your indexing business and marketing yourself as an indexer, and picks up from there.

Running an Indexing Business begins with an excellent overview, "The Business of Being in Business" (Pilar Wyman), followed by "Managing Your Moonlighting Business" (Carolyn Weaver)—a must-read. "Report from the Front Lines" (Dorothy DiRienzi) provides a description of the publishing world that indexers deal with almost daily. Chapters on independent contractor status (Kate Mertes) and setting fees (Jan Wright and Nan Badgett), a discussion on low-paying clients (Maria Coughlin), reprints of some *Key Words* columns on office space and project management (edited by Margie Towery), thoughts on using subcontractors (Enid L. Zafran), and "Tips for a Winning Proposal" and "Late Payment Blues" (Janet Perlman) round out the mix.

My thanks to my colleagues who contributed their time and intellectual labor to bring this book to life, and, of course, to my many friends and colleagues who have taught me, mentored me, and provided support over the years.

Janet Perlman
Editor

Contributors

Nan Badgett
Nan Badgett, owner of Word-a-bil-i-ty, has provided indexing services to publishers, authors and corporate clients since 1991. Nan was a founder of the Arizona Chapter of the ASI, and served as a chapter officer from 1994 to 1999.

Joanne Clendenen
Joanne Clendenen has been indexing on a freelance basis for five years, and, since early 2000, has been a technical document editor for a small consulting firm in Houston. In 1995, she founded the South Central Chapter of the ASI and has been its president and secretary off and on over the years since. She has also been part of a teaching team at the national level of the ASI, teaching a workshop on basic indexing every year since 1998. As a result of editing indexes for technical documents, she has launched herself on a mission to bring better quality indexing to the technical field. Her favorite subjects, though, are religion and myth, philosophy, history and social science.

Maria Coughlin
Maria Coughlin has been indexing for nearly 20 years and is president of Coughlin Indexing Services, Inc., where she has six associate indexers.

Dorothy DiRienzi
Dorothy DiRienzi has been in medical publishing for 35 years, as a copy editor, editorial manager, and indexer. She now works at Arizona State University as a full-time associate editor and does freelance indexing and editing through her company, Medit. Dorothy has been active in the Arizona ASI Chapter and serves as its president (1999-2001).

Anne Leach
Anne Leach has been a freelance indexer since 1985 and a member of ASI for the same period. She has been president of the Golden Gate and Southern California chapters, a member of the ASI Board for two consecutive three-year terms, chaired the Publicity Committee for three years while also serving on the Board, and was editor of *Key Words* for six years.

Kate Mertes
Kate Mertes earned her B.A. in Medieval Studies from Mount Holyoke College and a Ph.D. in Medieval English History from the University of Edinburgh (Scotland). After teaching at the university level, she moved into publishing. Kate has been indexing for over 20 years, starting with a fellow undergraduate's thesis. After stints with Oxford University Press and Andromeda Press in Britain, Kate returned to the United States in 1990. She is a freelance indexer and writes screenplays on the side.

Alexandra Nickerson
Alexandra Nickerson has been indexing since 1965. She specializes in medical and health-related materials and also indexes software applications, books, cookbooks, and textbooks. She has served the ASI as president (1997-1998), vice president, and a member of the board of directors. She served a three-year term as chair of the H.W. Wilson/ASI Award, a one-year term as chair of the Heartlands Chapter of the ASI, and a three-year term as chair of the Education Committee of the ASI. She has also been an instructor for the United States Department of Agriculture (USDA) Graduate School basic indexing course.

Janet Perlman
Janet Perlman has been indexing since 1967. Her company, Southwest Indexing, specializes in scientific, technical, and engineering materials, and also provides indexing for Spanish-language materials. Janet has a B.A. in Chemistry and a masters degree in Organizational Management. She has served ASI on the national level as Secretary and a Board member, and served on or chaired numerous national committees from 1994 to the present. Janet is a founder and officer of the Arizona ASI Chapter and has presented workshops on indexing. She is a frequent contributor to *Key Words*, and teaches indexing.

Marilyn Rowland
Marilyn Rowland has been an indexer for over 30 years and enjoys working in a wide range of subject areas and with different types of materials: books, periodicals, Web sites, and embedded indexes. She serves as Webmaster for a number of sites, including the Massachusetts Society of Indexers Web site. For fun, she writes, produces and directs local cable access television programs, and participates in several musical ensembles on Cape Cod, where she lives with her husband and two wonderfully talented children.

Sandi Schroeder
Sandi Schroeder started Schroeder Indexing Services in 1972 and provides indexing services for back-of-the-book projects, periodicals, and catalogs. She has employed staff as well as independent contractors. She served as president of the

Chicago/Great Lakes Chapter for 1996-1998; member of the national board of directors from 1995 to 1998; ASI vice president, 1998-1999; ASI president, 1999-2000; and is currently serving as past president.

Richard Shrout
Richard Shrout has been preparing indexes for computer books for over 10 years. He is the current chair of the DC ASI Chapter and has served two terms as secretary of that chapter.

Barbara Stroup
Barbara Stroup has a background as an audiologist and teacher of writing in educational and medical environments. She has been indexing for almost 10 years. Barbara has been president and treasurer of the Massachusetts Society of Indexers.

Margie Towery
Margie Towery has a graduate degree in history, attained after her daughters started school. In addition to experience in archival work and historical research, she has worked in publishing for over a decade and has been indexing for almost 10 years after finally discovering that indexing was what she wanted to do "when she grew up." She works primarily for scholarly presses and, while she considers herself a generalist, enjoys indexing books in social sciences, women's studies, history, sociology, and literary criticism. Her writing, including poetry and nonfiction, has been published in anthologies and academic venues. Margie's nonindexing life includes a passion (though little time) for quilting.

Carolyn Weaver
Carolyn Weaver was an academic medical librarian for 35 years (most recently at the University of Washington Health Sciences Library), began a second career moonlighting as an indexer of health and behavioral sciences books and journals in 1991, and as of February 2000 has made the transition to full-time indexing. She is in her second term as treasurer of the ASI and is a former president of the Pacific Northwest (PNW) Chapter/ASI, as well as the original listowner of Index-NW, the PNW/ASI discussion list. She lives and works in Bellevue, Washington, with one husband, two daughters, three cats, and a dog.

Jan C. Wright
Jan Wright is the owner of Wright Information Indexing Services, which has provided print and online indexing to companies such as Microsoft, Coriolis, Visio, PeachPit Press, and Alaska Northwest Publishing. She has a Master's Degree in Library Science and uses her many years of experience as a professional librarian to make more user-friendly indexes. She specializes in technical indexing and

information architecture for software companies. She is a member of the American Society of Indexers, and co-editor of *A to Z: The Newsletter of STC's Indexing SIG*.

L. Pilar Wyman

Pilar Wyman is a professional freelance indexer in Annapolis, Maryland. Her education includes a B.A. from St. John's College and two years' graduate study in Mathematics at the University of California, Berkeley. In 1983, she started work in indexing as a typist for a veteran indexer, and went solo in 1990. She is the editor of the ASI book publication *Indexing Specialties: Medicine*, and the current editor of the ASI bulletin *Key Words*. She is also an instructor for the USDA Basic Indexing and Advanced Indexing correspondence programs. Her specialties include clinical medicine and trade books.

Enid L. Zafran

Enid Zafran, who is the Director of Indexing Services at The Bureau of National Affairs in Washington, D.C., also has run her own indexing business, Indexing Partners, for more than a decade. She is the chair of the ASI's Publication Committee, has edited the book *Starting an Indexing Business (second edition)*, and contributed articles to the forthcoming book, *Indexing Specialties: Law*. She is a founding member of the Consortium of Indexing Professionals as well as a former member of the ASI Board.

Chapter 1

The Business of Being in Business

L. Pilar Wyman © 2001

Two aspects of being in business will be discussed: basic information about being in business, and "Burgeonings," which discusses expanding your business—whether to do it, how to do it, and how to manage it.

THE BASICS OF BEING IN BUSINESS

Finances

Now that you've got work, money is coming in. So are bills. Time for some bookkeeping! Filing systems come in many different shapes and sizes. You can sort your client files by whatever system works for you: by job, client, specialty, time, the solstices, whatever. But how you file your finances will consist of essentially two types of files: Accounts Receivable and Accounts Payable.

Accounts payable (payables)

Payables include paperwork for monies you owe. This means bills: Federal Express, courier services, America Online, telephone, *Publishers Weekly* subscriptions, ASI dues, insurance payments, software upgrades, etc. You will probably want to sort them by due date, and may even prefer to file them on your desktop versus in a desk drawer, so you can see them and keep track of them more efficiently. Once you've paid a bill, always keep the receipt. Receipts are important not only for general bookkeeping and in case of any inconsistencies or lost mail but also for tax purposes. Don't forget that business expenses are tax deductible. But we'll get into that later. You can file your receipts into expense folders, perhaps sorted by tax category (e.g., supplies, advertising, professional subscriptions, dues, e-mail fees), or by vendor.

Keeping track of your payables will help you determine your budget. *Budgeting* is critical so that you can make your payments on time. Budgeting is also pretty straightforward once you take a look at your bills critically. Many are monthly (telephone, e-mail, delivery services), or can be. Others you may pay less often, such as membership dues or disability insurance, but they can be broken down into monthly payments. Don't forget to allow for miscellaneous expenses, such as office supplies or other as-needed purchases.

Make sure you pay for your business expenses from a business checking account. Mixing pleasure and business is always inadvisable, especially when it comes to banking, so be sure to get a separate checking account for your business. Your lawyer and tax preparer will approve.

Accounts receivable (receivables)

Receivables include paperwork for monies due you. This is where you keep copies of the invoices you have sent out for jobs done. You'll probably want to do one folder for invoices you're awaiting payment on (Accounts Receivable), and one for those whose checks you have received (Income). Before you move an invoice from Receivables to Income make sure you mark on it the date payment was received. It is also helpful to staple any check stubs to the invoice copy. For quick summaries and easy tax computations, keep a record of income received. You'll want to note the date payment was received, the name of the client who sent the check, the original invoice total (what you billed), how much you put aside for taxes, and how much you received in total.

Invoices

What should your invoices look like? At a minimum, you should include all your usual business header information (name, address, telephone, etc.), your Social Security number, (or tax or employee identification number), the date, client contact information (name, address, etc.), job title, terms of payment (e.g., "Payment due upon receipt"), and amount due and your calculation (# of entries @ $/entry for example) including any delivery or other additional fees. See the end of this article for samples of invoices that work.

Taxes

What's kept you awake during this chapter are those scary, elusive references to taxes every now and then, yes? You've probably also heard that taxes for self-employed people are a bear. Well, you're right. But even if you are employed by someone else, you should still read this section. The deductions that a self-employed person can take are perfectly legitimate for an employee to take, under certain circumstances.

> **Disclaimer**: I am not a Certified Public Accountant (CPA) or tax consultant.
> **Caveat**: Always consult with a professional tax consultant.

As a self-employed person, you are responsible for all your taxes (Social Security, FICA, etc.), both the employer's and employee's shares. An employed person is responsible solely for the employee's share of any taxes. When you are self-employed, you are your own boss, in terms of who calls the shots and of who *pays* for them. Clearly, the self-employed person has to pay more.

The most important tax a freelance indexer must consider is the self-employment tax. The self-employment tax is how the federal government makes sure you are paying your share of those taxes that are usually the employer's responsibility. Generally, financial advisors recommend you deduct 15 percent from any income for this tax.

The Internal Revenue Services (IRS) requires that you pay your taxes quarterly, but they give you your first independent year as a grace period and will not fine you should you not pay the full amount you owe for that year as due quarterly. These are called Estimated Taxes.

When you first sit down to compute your taxes, determine what percentage of all your income you are paying to the IRS. Unless things change drastically in the coming year, it's a safe bet that you'll owe the same percentage the following year. After you have filed that first return, the IRS and your state comptroller's office will send you quarterly estimated tax forms. Estimated tax due dates are important—mark them on your calendar just like any other deadline. As each estimated tax due date approaches and you have determined what percentage of your income you owe, all you need to do is tally up how much you took in so far, multiply the total by the percentage you paid that year, and submit that amount to the IRS.

To be even better prepared, you'll want to make sure you have these funds on hand. As each check comes in, put aside a percentage of the funds for taxes. Remember the Accounts Receivable/Income form mentioned above? That form is an excellent way to keep track of how much you are making and how much you should submit to the IRS, both quarterly and yearly (the last quarter being due the same time as the year's total taxes). To make sure you don't mix the funds you've set aside for taxes, you may even want to consider a separate business savings account for those funds (Why not earn some interest while you're at it?).

Another item worthy of serious consideration is the home office deduction. The qualifications for a home office are often talked about in the media. Review the definition carefully in your tax materials. The IRS is the best source for this, as it is for *any* tax issues. While the chances of the IRS auditing you are slim (fewer than 4 percent of sole proprietors are audited in a year), you must work to comply with their regulations. Don't forget to consider items like telephone lines, either. If you want to deduct telephone expenses directly, then you will need a dedicated telephone line; otherwise, you will have to figure out your telephone expenses call by call.

The more experience you get doing your taxes, the more you will learn how to file efficiently. Some indexers use tools like Quicken or TurboTax to help file taxes. The more experience you get doing your taxes, the more you will learn what you can deduct, such as supplies.

Supplies

As you'll see on the tax forms, the types of professional supplies are varied. And now that you are at the point of earning enough to do taxes, you are also most likely at the point where you need more tools and supplies to help you work efficiently.

As the above section discussed, you may choose to use some sort of financial and/or tax preparation software. Additional packages for your software library include indexing software, word processing software, telecommunications/e-mail packages, and maybe time management or scheduling tools.

Besides your desktop computer and companion printer, additional equipment at this time includes a laptop computer for doing work while away from your home office (some say that you can always tell the freelancers from the in-house indexers at an indexing conference; the freelancers spend their free time in their hotel rooms working) and a fax machine. Even though your desktop computer/telecommunications software may have fax capability, the fax machine offers the benefits of quick copying facilities, answering machine capabilities, and the advantage of receiving faxes when your computer is not on. There will be plenty of times when your clients will need to fax you pages, or you'll want to fax them sample pages. Taking a break to go down to the corner office services store to use the fax machine—and to pay for that service—is not always convenient, so go ahead and take the plunge. In fact, many of the models available today use plain paper, which means you can even make plain-paper copies right at your desk. Fax copies may not be legally binding, and decay after a few months, so this may be a very worthwhile and time-saving advantage for some.

Other supplies you'll want to keep in stock include additional calendars, reference books, and all the miscellaneous items that belong on or near your desk. In fact, why not buy things in bulk now? You can save money in the long run, you've got the work to warrant the expense, and you will use them.

Work

> *I wonder whether there is any profession in which a knowledge of one's tongue is of the slightest use.*
>
> —T.E. Lawrence, on winning first place in English Language and Literature in the Senior Oxford Local Exams, 1906

Now that you've got work, take a minute to relax. Look around you. You are succeeding at being in business in indexing. You're spending your days doing what you enjoy. (If you don't enjoy it, get out!) Who's in first place now? You are!

Getting work

Never stop marketing. As hard as it may be, the most important time to market yourself, once your business is on its way, is while you are working. Marketing rarely gets you work right away, so to be sure you line up work for next July, you should consider making some calls or writing some letters *now*. Think you don't have time?

Make time! As you establish relationships with editors, chances are that you will occasionally be able to get work with a quick phone call; then again, you should never count on that phone call to get you work right away.

And though you will always follow the axiom that *Quality is Rule #1* when you do work, you also need to make sure that your clients do, too. The better your clients treat you, the better you will treat them and do your indexing for them. Are your contracts or indexing agreements complete? The more work you do, the greater your chances that you will encounter a "sticky" situation. This might mean a client takes a long time to pay you, a job takes longer than anticipated, or a job turns out to be larger than anticipated or disappears. All these situations can be prepared for, at least somewhat. While many indexers rely on verbal agreements and, indeed, such agreements are often sufficient, you will still want to use written agreements as much as possible. Some of your jobs will be one-shot deals, for example, for which you want as much protection as possible.

> *Free-lancing is like playing sandlot second base—*
> *the ball takes some awful hops.*
>
> —Ernest Hemingway

The ASI has a sample contract which is a good place to start. At minimum, your contract should include all your usual business header information (name, address, contact info, etc.), client contact information (name, address, etc.), date, job title and general project description (book index, newsletter indexer, database services, whatever), anticipated project length and/or deadline and date due, payment rates, and signature lines.

Some of your larger publishing clients may prefer you sign their own contract forms. Review them carefully and make sure you agree with the contents before signing.

It may also be worthwhile to have an attorney review any contract before you sign it. (*Note:* Some of your professional groups may have attorney services available to members at a nominal fee.) If you do experience problems with a client, the Better Business Bureau and the Small Business Administration are your best resources.

Doing work

A student recently asked me about continuing education for indexers. My response was that we learn on the job. The more you index, the more you will learn about indexing and about the topics you index. And the better you will index. Your reference books may become dog-eared and multiply, and highlighters may seem to always run dry, but these are only signs that your skills—like your work—are increasing.

> *Indexing work is not recommended to*
> *those who lack an orderly mind*
> *and a capacity for taking pains.*
> *A good index is a minor work of art*
> *but it is also the product of clear thought*
> *and meticulous care.*
>
> —Peter Farrell, *How to Make Money from Home*

Time management

A successful freelancer is dedicated to her work and structures her time accordingly. Scheduling systems come in a variety of colors, shapes, and sizes, but anyone who is successful has one, and most likely swears by his or her system.

One consistent element of any system that works is a "tickler file." A tickler file is where/how you keep track of things to do and things that you are currently doing. You might use a folder and label it "Jobs in Progress," or you might use a blank lined book, or you might use a combination of methods. Whatever method you choose doesn't matter, as long as it works for you.

You also have to determine what method of scheduling your time works best. By now you should have an idea of how much time you need to complete an average job. The question becomes how to carve out that time best. Are you at your best in the mornings or in the evenings? Whenever you are at your best is when you should work. Schedule your day so that is when you are working.

Perhaps you need steady daycare to tend to your children so you can work during prime hours. Perhaps you need to switch the house telephone line answering machine to auto-answer. Perhaps you need to tell your mother not to call until after working hours. Don't be surprised if you have to make some effort to maintain your schedule. This is called being *on deadline*.

Soon it will seem as if you are *always* on deadline!

BURGEONINGS (EXPANDING YOUR BUSINESS, OR NOT)

You have so much work, you don't know what to do. To paraphrase the great bard, "To expand or not to expand, that is the question." You have two options; you can say, "Yes" to more work, or you can say, "No." Following are scenarios in response to each answer. But before you answer the question of whether to increase or not, be sure to consider what you want for your business and for yourself. This requires serious reflection. Make sure you maintain your business as *you* see fit.

Finances

Financially, you will know you're at the crossroads of growth when you have made enough money and then some consistently. You know you're making enough money because you have more money coming in than you need. You know this because, over time, you have seen that your payables—both business and personal—only require a certain amount of money each month, and, after taxes, you've got that (you might even be consistently ahead a month or two). You know this because you have consistently met your budget. You know this because you have paid your taxes easily for a few years now, and see that there is nothing more that you need to purchase, really, beyond a certain amount each year.

Saying No

If you choose No to more work, then you have chosen to maintain your income as is—growing with inflation, of course, but no more. You will have also chosen to keep your expenses no higher than they currently are. This means that if you don't need to get a new desk, then you will turn a blind eye to that beautiful cherry one you saw at the antique store yesterday. You can also opt to increase your rates, so as to best preserve your net income. With inflation and the cost of living increasing consistently, you will need to raise your rates. Increasing your rates can also help you keep a handle on your work, and make sure that you are compensated fairly for your time and expertise, especially as your expertise increases.

Saying Yes

If you choose Yes to more work, then you may have to consider enlarging your business. Be responsible! If you take on more work than you can actually do, then you will need to hire some others to help you complete the work and meet the deadlines. You can do this a couple of ways:

- You can subcontract the work to other indexers.
- You can hire student interns. Does your local college or university have a library school or technical communications program? Give them a call. Compensation for students who participate includes educational credits versus money.
- You can hire employees and train them.

Hiring others as employees requires becoming an employer. The tax implications are complicated. Review your tax materials and definitions carefully. You may even want to consult with a CPA. As an employer you will be obligated to provide salaries and regular compensation of some sort to your employees. *It is illegal to do otherwise.* You will also be obligated to fulfill various tax requirements (the employer's share of Social Security and FICA taxes, for example), and payroll taxes. You will also need to provide your employees with workspace. Your home office may no longer suffice.

Subcontracting to others does not entail quite as many tax considerations as hiring employees, though you would still be required to provide your subcontractors with 1099-M (Miscellaneous Income) forms. These are the forms you receive as a subcontractor from your clients, and which the IRS requires for *any* work over $600.

In some cases, whether you hire subcontractors or employees or interns, or not, you may want to consider incorporating your business. Self-incorporation is a way to keep your taxes low though your income may increase. Instead of paying self-employment taxes on all your business income, you put yourself on a minimal salary and pay self-employment taxes on the difference only. Even this method, however, will require more paperwork and tax preparation fees.

No matter how you do it, as you expand your business, your expenses will increase. Fulfilling all these tax and work requirements entails time, materials, and money. Be careful.

Work

You will know you're at the crossroads of growth when you face more work than you can handle, or merely the prospect of more work than you can handle. There are only so many working hours in the week, and you need to have a life beyond indexing, after all. "How to keep a life?" becomes the question.

Getting work

The question of getting work is not moot, however. In fact, getting work and marketing is *never* done. The publishing industry is in constant flux. Editors come and go, and as comfortable as you may feel with clients, you must always be prepared for the prospect of indexing without them. You must continually prepare for the possibility of not having work. Remember: Just because you have work this week, doesn't mean that you will six weeks from now. Just because you are established now doesn't mean you get to stop marketing yourself.

> *The essence of the freelance life is freedom. Idleness is part of freedom and shouldn't alarm you: You will find soon enough that you have more than enough on your plate. Relish these periods of rest. To be a freelancer, it is also necessary to believe, to know, to know profoundly, that one is going to be all right however unlikely it seems at any particular distressing moment. This faith your friends cannot give you: It is something you have to discover in yourself.*
>
> —V.S. Naipul, to Paul Theroux, June 6, 1972

Saying No

The difference now is that you can target your audience all the more selectively. In the beginning of your career you may have sent your resume to every person whose name and address you could find, yet once your business was up and running you may have targeted only those in your fields of specialty and expertise. Now you need go after only those you are really interested in or those whose topics truly whet your appetite. Choosing to keep your workload down allows you the luxury of picking and choosing what jobs to take and what clients to go after.

Saying Yes

Choosing to continue to increase your workload means that you can continue to market yourself both generally and specifically. You can go after the clients whose work you are genuinely interested in, charity and pro bono cases even (these could be tax deductions, remember), if you want, as well as others. As you continue to earn more, your budget for marketing (also tax deductible as it's a business expense, don't forget) should also grow.

Perhaps now is the time for a Web site if you haven't already. The benefits of a Web site are not just marketing and exposure. Getting tired of sending out copies of your resume or lists of titles indexed? Direct the caller to your Web site, where it's all sitting nice and pretty, ready for downloading.

Perhaps now is the time for a brochure or a newsletter. Be creative. And don't forget all the previous marketing strategies you've developed. Whatever strategies worked for you before will probably continue to be fruitful. Marketing and advertising are strategies that are always important to a business, no matter what stage of the business life cycle you are in.

Doing work

Saying No

If you decide No to the work, then you have to consider how you will say it—as politely as possible—and you have to consider which jobs you will say it to. Picking and choosing what work you will do is sometimes fun, as you may get to choose topics or projects that interest you. But you will still have to go for those jobs which, while you may not be that keen on them, will fill that hole in your schedule, and it is for an employer whose projects you generally enjoy, after all.

For some indexers, No may mean working 10 months out of the year, and then "taking it easy" for the rest of year as they have earned all they need to earn. For other indexers, No may mean working six hours a day, while the children are in school, for example, and taking it easy over holidays and school breaks. For other indexers, No may mean working full-time, eight hours a day, and taking it easy over traditional holidays and on scheduled vacations.

Saying Yes

If you decide Yes to the work, then you have to consider how you will do it. When will you do it? Weekends? Nights? If you don't do it, who will? A subcontractor? A protégé? An employee? An intern?

This raises the issue of quality control. Since *Quality is Rule #1* can never be forgotten, especially if you want clients to call you back. Can you be sure that jobs that go out with your name on them meet your standards? Consider carefully how you will control quality. Will you review each job that goes out? Perhaps you're interested in training indexers to work for you. Perhaps you can schedule jobs based on your employees' areas of expertise and interest (not to mention your own). Put together some checklists for yourself and for your employees to complete at the end of each job.

Time management

As with all scheduling, no matter the size of the business, the trick is to rely on whatever system works best for you.

Saying No

If you decide to keep your workload and business size as is, then you may not need to change your time management methods. On the other hand, you really can't let yourself get complacent. We humans are constantly growing and changing, and a method that works fine for you today may not tomorrow.

Saying Yes

If you decide to increase your workload and/or business, then you will also need to increase your time management efforts. Hiring others, however you choose to do so, will require additional time commitments on your part. You will have to take time to interview prospective employees, train your employees, schedule their work, and review their work. Whether you choose to hire others or to work with subcontractors, apprentices, or interns, tracking jobs becomes trickier with increased work. In some cases, you will be working on more than one job at a time, which will require flowsheets of some sort. In other cases, you will have more than one person working on a job (or more), which will also require flow-charting. Some indexers even tap employees for scheduling and have one person in charge of all scheduling to best coordinate workflow.

EPILOGUE: THE BOONS OF BEING IN BUSINESS IN INDEXING

The benefits of being in business in indexing are numerous:

- working with books and words everyday
- intellectual challenges
- constant learning
- flexibility
- financial independence

- freedom to plan your work yourself
- freedom to organize your time yourself
- freedom from control by others
- work ownership

RESOURCES

Here are some additional information sources for indexers in business for themselves.

> Folger, Liz. "Home Business Profile: Indexer,"*The Stay-At-Home Mom's Guide to Making Money: How to Create the Business That's Right for You Using the Skills and Interests You Already Have.* Prima Publishing. 1997. p. 187.
>
> Gardner, Larry. *Simple Steps to Job Success.* Graduate School Press. 1994. Available from the U.S. Department of Agriculture, Washington, D.C. 20250.
>
> Harrison, Larry and L. Pilar Wyman. "Indexing FAQ (Frequently Asked/Answered Questions) File" at the American Society of Indexers Web site: http://www.asindexing.org. NetGuide says, this "extensive FAQ file covers the art of the practice, as well as the prosaic questions of salary, freelancing, and building a clientele."
>
> *Home Office Computing* magazine. Their Web site is http://www.smalloffice.com.
>
> "2000 Professional Activities and Salary Survey," American Society of Indexers. The Web Site is http://www.asindexing.org.
>
> Small Business Administration, 409 3rd St., SW, Room 6400, Washington, DC 20416. Tel: 202-205-6665 or 1-800-9-ASK-SBA. The Web site is http://www.sbaonline.sba.gov.
>
> *Tips For Successful Freelancing.* Editorial Freelancers Association. 1992. Available from EFA publications, 71 West 23rd Street, Suite 1504, New York, NY 10010. Their Web site is http://www.the-efa.org.

Portions of this chapter previously appeared in Key Words, *Vol. 6, Issue 2, March/April 1998.*

Chapter 2

Managing Your Moonlighting Business

Carolyn G. Weaver © 2001

*Moonlighting: The practice of holding a
second regular job in addition to one's main job*

"What do you do?"

When that question comes up in a social context, the answer is not simple for the moonlighting indexer. Do you reply that you're a librarian/technical writer/grocery checker who also indexes? Or, do you announce that you have a part-time indexing business in addition to a full-time job? Full-time indexers must often explain to friends and family what an indexer does and may have to justify why they can't be the on-the-block emergency backup for every working parent in the neighborhood since they have the freedom to work reasonable hours (deadlines permitting) and decide how to manage their own days. The moonlighting indexer, in contrast, spends eight hours at the day job and then goes home to a second career—not only to writing and editing indexes, but also to all the myriad details required for running a business—marketing, billing and collections, paying taxes, record-keeping, etc. The only difference between moonlighting and running a full-time indexing business is the amount of time available for your business.

By definition, a self-employed moonlighter is one who holds a second job in addition to his or her primary one and who pursues that second occupation without long-term commitments to any one employer. More specifically for the purposes of this discussion, moonlight indexing is pursued systematically and on a businesslike basis as a sideline to another full-time position. A part-time indexer with another part-time salaried position also qualifies as a moonlighter if there is potential for conflict of interest between the two part-time jobs and if the salaried position makes serious inroads into the time available for indexing. Part-time indexing, which is one's sole occupation and deliberately limited to less than full time by choice, is not moonlighting; it is simply a part-time job. Nor does an occasional index done as a favor to a friend or to satisfy professional obligations qualify as moonlighting; in that context, indexing is an avocation rather than a profession.

The key factors that differentiate moonlighting from a hobby or other part-time employment are the following: (1) Indexing is treated by the practitioner as a business; (2) the time available to pursue the moonlight endeavor is limited; and (3) the potential for conflict of interest exists with another position. This chapter will focus especially on the conflict of interest issues, as well as moonlighting survival techniques. Finally, we'll briefly explore the factors that determine when it's time to either move to full-time indexing or call it quits as a moonlighter.

REALITY CHECK FOR MOONLIGHTING

Before you embark on a moonlighting career, ask yourself the following questions:
- Will your moonlighting be a business or a hobby?
- Which job will be the main one: your day job or the one that begins after the dishes are done and the kids are in bed? (Don't forget which one pays the mortgage!)
- What are your goals as a moonlighter? How will you measure success?
- Are you willing to work seven-day weeks, 52 weeks out of the year? Vacations and holidays do not exist for a moonlighter; your only days off are the ones when pages fail to arrive on schedule.
- Is your family or significant other supportive of your goals?

If you have realistic answers to the first three questions and can honestly answer "Yes" to the last two, you're ready to start moonlighting.

MOONLIGHTING INDEXING IS A BUSINESS, NOT A HOBBY!

By viewing indexing as a hobby rather than a business, you can avoid many of the complications of moonlighting, accepting only those paid or volunteer indexing projects that conveniently fit into your schedule. Start-up costs will be minimal since it's unlikely that you will invest heavily in software or equipment in order to write one or two indexes a year. Avocational income is reported as miscellaneous to the various tax agencies, and you can still deduct business expenses from your gross income, but you need not be concerned with active marketing or juggling personal commitments to meet client expectations.

A moonlighting business, in contrast, requires the same initial investment and proportional amount of effort as running a full-time business. This includes obtaining all the necessary business licenses (city, state, and local) for your area and establishing a business identity through the use of business cards and letterhead, telephone number, checking account, and e-mail and Web addresses distinct from those of your full-time employer. Successful moonlighting requires an investment in professional indexing software and business equipment, as well as acquiring the training and experience necessary to provide top-quality professional services to clients. As with any business, services must be actively marketed, all client commitments must be met, and normal business management activities must be performed. Since the amount of time available to devote to indexing is limited, an ethical moonlighter will accept only those jobs can be completed in the time available. When schedules slip (which they will!) or equipment fails, the moonlighter must have a contingency plan in place—backup equipment, accrued vacation time, and colleagues to call on for support—to cover the crisis. Successful moonlighters don't miss deadlines!

The day job must not get shortchanged!

For most moonlighters, the day job pays the bills and the fringe benefits. It must not be neglected! For 40 hours a week, the moonlighter's full-time employer is entitled to 100 percent of his or her efforts. Just as the demands of the day job do not constitute an acceptable excuse for missing indexing deadlines, the fact that one was up until 3 a.m. the previous night finishing an index is not an acceptable reason for arriving late at work or failing to turn in a report on time. The moonlighter should expect no special considerations from either indexing clients or full-time employer; his or her moonlighting status is a personal choice.

MOTIVES FOR MOONLIGHTING

Personal motives for moonlight indexing should be weighed against both the advantages and the disadvantages of simultaneously maintaining two careers. Major *advantages* include:

- You can try out indexing as a career, with the security of a regular paycheck.
- Your employer provides benefits (health insurance, social security, disability).
- You get tax breaks (deductions for home office, business equipment, software, second phone lines, office supplies, and professional memberships and travel), most of which are not deductible by an employee without an outside business.
- Your employer supports your professional travel and participation in professional activities.
- You build up a client base in preparation for going full-time. Day job contacts can lead to indexing jobs as long as one avoids conflict of interest.
- You have the perfect excuse for ignoring housework!

The *disadvantages* may be less apparent:

- You have less free time. Expect to use the vacation from your day job to meet indexing deadlines. Assume that any three-day holiday weekend from your day job simply offers another day for indexing. Be pleasantly surprised when you really *do* get time off!
- Your additional income may move you to a higher tax bracket.
- Moonlighting conflicts with the demands of your full-time job. Since your day job pays the bills and the benefits, the indexing schedule must factor in your employer's deadlines.

- Moonlighting will have an impact on family and social life. Just remember to factor your sister's wedding and your son's high school graduation into the indexing schedule!

Anyone considering a career as an indexer has a number of options: (1) obtain a salaried or contract position working for someone else; (2) index occasionally as an avocation, with no intention of making it a business; (3) moonlight while maintaining the security and benefits of a full-time day job; or (4) plunge in as a full-time freelancer, with sufficient personal resources to keep afloat until the business takes off. None of these categories is exclusive, and one may progress from one stage to another. My career is typical. My first paid journal index in 1983 was done as a favor to a library patron, with no intention of generating significant income. Eight years later, I began moonlighting and maintained that status until my children were through college; in 2000, I made the transition to full-time indexer.

My personal motives for becoming a moonlighter were straightforward: two daughters approaching college age, inadequate savings, and little prospect for financial aid. In addition, I had a long-range vision for my post-retirement years of sitting at a picnic table in Olympic National Park, indexing on a laptop computer while watching the gray whales migrating offshore. My moonlighting goals were to generate the additional income needed for my daughters' college expenses, while acquiring the client base, experience, and pension funding needed to make that full-time vision possible within 10 years—a scenario that was achieved on schedule. My personal measure of success as a moonlighter was to have all the work I could handle on a part-time basis and regularly turn down work for lack of time.

Moonlighting requires a significant commitment on the part of both the indexer and his or her family, since it sharply reduces the amount of free time available for other activities. Regardless of your motives—additional income, building a hedge against unemployment in an era of corporate downsizing, testing the waters before making a career change, dissatisfaction with the day job, preparation for a new career after retirement—the indexer's motives and measures of success should be clearly understood by everyone affected, since a family "buy in" will make the indexer's moonlighting lifestyle immeasurably easier.

As a moonlighter, I typically averaged about 20 hours a week in indexing-related activities. When working on a project I normally indexed two to three hours per night Monday through Thursday, plus 12 to 18 hours on weekends. Between projects, evening hours were spent on preparing bids, bookkeeping, filing, identifying potential clients, and the myriad other details of running a business. Back-to-back projects meant that I might have no time off for weeks at a time; so, I learned to schedule in downtime and to take advantage of those rare free weekends for mundane activities such as yard work, camping trips, overdue personal correspondence, and catching up on sleep.

ETHICAL ISSUES

A major concern for any moonlighter who does not care to find himself or herself involuntarily thrown into full-time freelancing due to the loss of the day job will be to protect the security of the salaried position. If your day job is totally unrelated in any way to indexing, information science, academia, or publishing (e.g., you're an actor, a bricklayer, or a merchant seaman) you probably have nothing to worry about, provided your freelance activities do not affect your performance in the salaried position. For everyone else, however, a possible conflict of interest always exists.

It is, therefore, best to be up-front with your employer about your outside activities and to take positive steps to convince him or her that moonlighting will not affect your performance. The employer may see potentials for conflict of interest or misuse of company resources in all the following areas; so, be prepared to address all of these issues below.

Clear conflict of interest (illegal for public sector employees)

- You use employer's resources (office, staff, stationery, etc.) for private gain.
- You use employer's phone number, e-mail address, and/or fax number on your business cards, letterhead, or promotional materials.
- You offer a service in direct competition with the employer.
- You use employer-furnished e-mail, phone, faxes, copiers, computers for private gain (may be possible to use certain services if costs are reimbursed; get conditions in writing).

Fuzzy areas (get agreements in writing)

- You use vacation and sick leave to meet indexing deadlines. Under what circumstances will this be requested/permitted?
- You make and receive phone calls from clients during business hours. Is this ever permitted?
- You meet with clients during the day. Will you or won't you?
- You are reimbursed for professional expenses (e.g., attending ASI meetings). Will employer consider ASI participation a relevant professional activity?
- You have conflicting deadlines between employer and indexing projects: which has priority?
- You market to employer's clients. Assuming your service is not in competition with the employer's, to what extent may you market to your company's clients?

Finally, complete any conflict of interest forms required by your employer. This is absolutely essential for any public sector position, since failure to disclose outside activities may be grounds for dismissal. If tempted to hide your outside activities from your employer, remember that a cover-up that brought down the Nixon administration and not the illegal activities themselves!

MOONLIGHTING PROBLEMS AND SOLUTIONS

The moonlighting indexer has unique problems in running a business because his or her indexing business hours begin after his or her clients go home; all business activities are conducted in addition to a full day or week at the other job. The following are major areas of concern for most moonlighters, along with some suggestions for dealing with them.

Communicating with clients

The moonlighter, like all freelancers, must be easily accessible to potential clients during the day, since according to more than one editor, "The indexer who answers the phone is the one who gets the job." Although some business phone calls and e-mail messages will inevitably be handled during the day, they must be as discrete as possible, and with little or no impact on the day job's performance.

Telephone

The **business phone number** is the moonlighter's primary contact with clients. You should *never* use your full-time employer's phone number or address on business cards or stationery, in a brochure, or in other promotional materials for your private business. To do so is illegal for public employees. If you have a private phone line with voicemail at work, you can use call forwarding to transfer calls from your business line to your office number. As a moonlighter, I use a cellular phone as my business line and forward the calls to my current location (office phone during the week and to my home number evenings and weekends), so I am never out of contact with my clients. Under my cellular service plan, I am not charged for forwarded calls answered on a regular phone, so I rarely pay more than the basic monthly charge, which is a tax-deductible business expense. The volume of client calls was small enough that it is was not a concern for my employer. By call forwarding to my office line, I was also able to use "extended absence" greetings on voicemail to let all callers (including indexing clients) know when I was on vacation or otherwise unavailable, something I would never do on my home answering machine. As a full-time indexer, I continue to use the cell phone as my business number, since it allows clients to reach me when I am away from my home office.

If you do not have a private phone line at work, you should subscribe to private voicemail, use an answering machine, or hire an answering service to handle your calls rather than receiving personal business calls through a company operator or expecting other employees to take messages. Your client contacts should not have an impact on company operations at any level. If you check your answering system regularly (at least twice a day) and return calls promptly, clients never need know you are at your day job.

Use a personal calling card to pay for all personal long-distance calls made at work, which also creates a record for tax purposes and provides evidence if you are ever challenged as to potential misuse of resources; do not user your employer's

WATS line for business calls unless your employer agrees to such in writing. To the extent possible, return calls before and after work, during lunch hours, and on coffee breaks. This can also produce cost savings by taking advantage of non-peak phone rates in calling different time zones.

E-mail

Employer-furnished e-mail is a business resource which may be subject to conflict of interest legislation. While many companies will not object to limited personal use of corporate e-mail accounts on your own time, there will probably be significant concerns about use of a company e-mail address for private gain. Do verify your employer's policy concerning private use of company-provided e-mail for business purposes, subscriptions to listservs, and Web browsing. Also, remember that no e-mail message sent from your office computer *or from your company-provided e-mail account outside the office* is private. Your employer has the legal right to monitor your e-mail and Web surfing using its resources.

All moonlighters need a private e-mail address separate from any services supplied by their employers that can be used on business cards, letterheads, and in marketing. Use your private account exclusively for indexing-related communications, and do not be tempted to send a quick response to a client from your employer's account, unless your employer specifically permits such activities. If you use an e-mail system at work such as Outlook Express that allows access to multiple accounts, you may be able to access your personal e-mail from your office, but do verify company policies before loading any software on your office computer or accessing your private account from work.

Faxes and photocopies

One of the major benefits of moonlighting is that you have access to all the business equipment such as fax machines and photocopiers that may not fit into your personal budget, which is why use of that easily abused equipment by moonlighters may be carefully scrutinized by employers.

Do come to a clear understanding with your employer as to what is permissible with regard to the use of company equipment for personal use. If you work in a library or other institution that offers fee-based photocopy or fax services to clients, you can probably use those services for your business, provided that you pay for them at the same rates charged to any other client. If your company does not offer such services to the public, use your employer's fax number on your business card only if your employer agrees to such use in writing; assume that all photocopies and long-distance faxes must be reimbursed. A fax modem is an excellent investment.

Correspondence

Express mail fees are one of the largest recurring business expenses for most freelancers. Check out the various services, comparing not only regular fees but also pickup and delivery schedules and costs for special services such as Saturday delivery. One consideration for moonlighters in choosing a service is convenience for personal drop-off of packages. A Federal Express or Airborne Express drop box conveniently located on your regular commuting route can save time and provide an alternative to paying an additional fee for pickup of packages at your home or office.

Since most freelancers will have personal stationery for correspondence, use of the employer's letterhead for business use is not a consideration. However, you may be tempted to whip off a quick note to a client while at work, or (for librarians, especially) to do project-related research on company time. Don't do it. Your employer's time belongs to him or her. For those just starting moonlighting, it may take a certain amount of time to shift gears between your different roles. Remember which hat you are wearing in dealing with clients. Never sign a letter or an e-mail message to a client using your day job title, or imply in writing that your indexing activities are performed under the auspices of your full-time employer, and be careful when mentioning your day job in resumes and indexing-related promotional materials not to imply that indexing is done under the auspices of the day job.

In person

Since proximity to clients is not a requirement for freelance indexing, it is likely that most of your contacts with clients will be by phone or e-mail. However, sooner or later someone will want to meet with you in person, so it is best to discuss this eventuality with your employer and agree in advance as to what is permissible. For moonlighters, the best choice is to meet with clients on their own turf and to avoid meeting with indexing clients at the employer's place of business. Use vacation time, schedule meetings over lunch, or make up the time, but never solicit business on company time.

Time management

Efficient time management is critical for the moonlighter who is trying to manage a business in addition to a full-time job and the demands of family and friends. The key factor is to estimate jobs based on the amount of time you have available (not just the time required to do the index), and to recognize that while you may be able to index as fast as a full-time indexer, you cannot always provide the same turnaround time. For instance, I learned early in my moonlighting career that I should realistically expect to index no more than 200 pages (average size and subject density) a week while maintaining a full-time job. I, thus, requested a minimum of three weeks to index a 600-page book. This standard is, of course, flexible, but my experience with one 800-page book finished in three weeks (averaging about three hours of sleep a night) is a constant reminder of the importance of accepting only reasonable deadlines. Be honest with clients, and turn down work if you cannot reasonably expect to meet the deadline with nerves and other commitments intact. Develop a network of other indexers to whom you can confidently refer projects that you lack the time to accept. Recognize that refusing a client's project is better than accepting it and failing to deliver a quality product on schedule.

In accepting jobs, keep in mind potential conflicts with your employer's deadlines. Even if you have considerable flexibility in scheduling time off from your full-time job to complete projects, never *assume* that you will always be able to use vacation time for indexing. Your employer may look askance at a request for time off during the busiest time of the year or when he or she is waiting for the annual budget or a major report. Maintain a master calendar with all of your critical dates—work deadlines, personal and professional commitments, as well as scheduled indexes—and make sure that the "hole" is large enough before you schedule another project.

Remember to schedule downtime. A moonlighter can easily get so caught up in indexing that personal life disappears. Keep some of your weekends free, even if it means turning down an occasional job. On your master calendar, schedule in time for your family, a social life, and a vacation without work. Recognize that attending your 10-year-old's school play, walking on the beach with your spouse, or visiting an aging relative is just as important as indexing; leave time for it!

A moonlighter, even more than most working parents, may be tempted to be supermom or superdad since indexing takes even more time away from the family. Resist the temptation. Accept the reality that store-bought cookies are not indicative of a bad parent, and that dust bunnies make great low-maintenance pets. Recognize that it is less expensive to pay a housecleaning service to mop the floors than to take time from indexing to do it yourself (unless you consider floor mopping to be recreational). Also, a family that recognizes the value of moonlighting to its economic welfare will be far more supportive of your efforts. My husband routinely takes over all the weekend shopping when I'm in indexing mode, and my younger daughter was at one point paid to do the weekly housecleaning. In short, don't do it if it isn't necessary, and pay for the support services that you hate, whether housecleaning or accounting, especially if doing it yourself will cost more in terms of indexing income than the cost of paying someone else.

Financial matters

Because moonlighters have multiple sources of income and deductible business expenses, they must pay especially careful attention to financial recordkeeping. Do maintain a separate checking account (and perhaps a credit card) to track business-related income and expenses. Also, moonlighters can often avoid the hassle of filing estimated tax returns simply by increasing the amount of tax withheld by the full-time employer. Just be sure that the amount withheld is sufficient to avoid tax penalties from under-withholding.

It is important to recognize that under current U.S. tax laws, a business expenditure is more valuable for tax purposes than an itemized professional expense, since it reduces the gross profit subject to self-employment tax. For example, annual ASI dues and costs of attending the ASI annual conference, regardless of indexing income, can be deducted from your taxable profit as an indexing business expense on IRS Schedule C, reducing your taxable gross income by the amount of the deduction; you can deduct those itemized expenses on Schedule B only if your total professional expenses exceeds the minimum threshold. Direct costs of producing income (office supplies, a second phone line, computing equipment if used exclusively for your business, etc.) are also deductible as business expenses whether or not you claim a home office deduction. Talk to your tax advisor for details.

All of this leads to the big decision for moonlighters, which is whether to claim the home office as a deduction. As a moonlighter, you will probably be able to claim the home office deduction, provided that your home office is a separate and identifiable area within your home that is used regularly and exclusively as the principal work location for your indexing business (i.e., not also used for your day job). If you qualify, you can deduct a portion of the overhead costs of operating your home office—mortgage, utilities, major repairs—in addition to direct business expenses. In recent years, many self-employed individuals, particularly those with salaried employment, have avoided claiming this substantial financial benefit through fear that it will attract an IRS audit. In my opinion, assuming you are declaring all income and attempting to comply with the law to the best of your ability, it should be claimed if it qualifies. The exception is for those who move frequently or expect to sell their homes within two years, since there are tax implications at the time the house is sold. Again, talk to your tax advisor.

Relations with employer

I cannot stress enough the importance of maintaining good relations with your full-time employer. Be up-front with your employer about your outside activities, and resist the temptation to misuse vacation and sick leave. If concerned about a potential conflict of interest, discuss the situation with your employer. If a conflict occurs, you will avoid legal pitfalls; if your employer agrees the activity is appropriate, your integrity will be appreciated.

To insure support for your outside activities, put your indexing skills to work for your employer. Could your office procedures manual or company newsletter use an index? Volunteer to index it, using your software if necessary, on company time. Is there a project that can use your indexing expertise in subject control or organization? Position yourself as the staff expert on indexing-related matters. If your indexing skills are adding to the company's bottom line, there should be little resistance to letting you keep those skills up-to-date on your own time.

For many of those in academic institutions, participation in professional organizations is required for advancement and merit review. Your employer may provide encouragement, financial support, and release time for attending local and national ASI meetings, for writing and research, and for other participation. At the same time, you will be developing professional contacts and gaining information that may benefit your employer as well as yourself.

Look for opportunities to "double-dip"

Let your colleagues at work know that you are an indexer since jobs may be referred from anyone. While you cannot ethically market your services to your employer's clients, an inquiry at the reference desk about indexing may get referred to you. Casual conversation with a secretary about her boss's book in progress may identify you as an indexer and lead to an after-hours discussion of your services. Also, have a supply of your indexing business cards available at all times. Cards handed out to exhibitors at professional meetings may often lead to follow-up calls at a later date.

When is it time to quit or move to full-time indexing?

Moonlighting, for most freelancers, is a temporary rather than a long-term commitment. For some, the choice may be to quit indexing when the pressures of juggling two hats becomes overwhelming. Those trying out indexing as a profession may decide it's not for them. A promotion or an interesting new assignment at work may leave no time for moonlighting or cause one to decide to drop indexing back to hobby status. Or, a layoff at work may force an involuntary change to full-time freelancing as an alternative to seeking another salaried position.

For moonlighters with long-term, stable salaried positions, however, the thought of trading the security of a regular paycheck and associated fringe benefits for the economic instability of freelancing can be terrifying. When you have achieved your personal goals as a moonlighter, following are some of the indications that you are emotionally and financially ready to make the transition to full-time indexing:

- You think of yourself as an indexer who has a second job.
- You have all the work you can handle on a part-time basis and are regularly turning down indexing projects for lack of time.
- You have a core group of clients who regularly give you work.
- You have built networking relationships in the ASI and your local chapter and can count on referrals from your colleagues.
- Your personal resources—savings, line of credit, and family—can support you through the slow times.

And most important:

- Giving up indexing is unthinkable!

CONCLUSION

In conclusion, it is possible to survive moonlighting on a long-term basis with your health, reputation, full-time job, marriage, and sanity all intact. The key factor is to keep your various lives separate and to remember which hat your are wearing at the moment. Consider the needs and concerns of your spouse or significant other, your children, and your full-time employer, and involve them in your decision-making. Develop a reliable indexing support network to which you can refer clients when you are unable to accept a project, and remember that it is better for your professional reputation to turn down a job than to do it poorly or fail to meet a deadline.

Finally, keep your moonlighting goals in mind, and update them regularly. Your measures of success may be very different from those of another and may have nothing to do with your income. Whether yours is a short-term (to pay for a new car or a family vacation) or long-term (to prepare for a second career after retirement) goal, you're a success when you achieve those personal goals.

TEN COMMANDMENTS OF MOONLIGHTING

1. Thou shalt not attempt to conceal thy freelance business from thy employer, for such is the path to the unemployment agency.
2. Thou shalt not use thy employer's computer, telephone, fax machine, photocopier, office supplies, or e-mail account in connection with thy freelance business.
3. Thou shalt recognize thy personal limitations and accept only those jobs that thou canst realistically expect to finish on schedule. Moonlighters do not index 1,000-page books in a week.
4. Thou shalt not miss deadlines of either thy employer nor thy clients. Remember which job pays the mortgage and schedule indexing jobs accordingly.
5. Thou shalt not accept any indexing job which presents a conflict of interest with thy employer's business.
6. Thou shalt comply with all local and state rules for small business operation and shall maintain records sufficient to satisfy the IRS, keeping thy business and personal finances separate.
7. Thou shalt network with other indexers and become active in the ASI and other professional associations, for such is the sources of referrals.
8. Thou shalt schedule time with thy family and friends and recognize that an indexing lull is a treasure to be prized for marketing, recreation, or sleep.
9. Thou shalt regard dust bunnies as pets.
10. Thou shalt know when to say "NO!"

Chapter 3

Report from the Front Lines

Dorothy DiRienzi © 2001

A discussion about how print production editors commission back-of-the-book indexes and getting a glimpse into their environment might help indexers who have never been in the trenches to understand such concepts as:

- The publishing chain of command
- Responsibilities of the production team
- Scheduling and publishing deadlines
- Assigning work to freelancers
- Purchase orders, letters of agreement, contracts
- Publishers' specs
- Communication during the job and author contacts
- Invoicing
- Follow-ups

WHO'S IN CHARGE

The title "editor" applies to a variety of job descriptions in a publishing house. This discussion highlights only those positions that affect a freelance indexer or editor. Of course, remember that reviewing the activities of all these positions are an editorial board, an army of accountants, the board of directors, and the shareholders. Decisions made down the line are ultimately influenced by how these other entities perceive the track records of all the other editors.

Usually, an **executive editor** or an **acquisitions editor** is responsible for finding an author and nailing down the contract; this person is also responsible for drawing up the initial budget for producing and marketing the book and for estimating its profitability for the house.

These initial negotiations set the stage for some of the parameters that affect freelancers, such as who will pay for the index (the author, through deductions to royalties or right up front, the publishing house, or a split between the two) and how much influence the author will be allowed to exert during production (how often and how much he or she will be allowed to fiddle with proofs and/or index). Depending on the book's budget, the decision is made to produce it through the publisher's in-house facilities (i.e., production group) or to farm it out to a "packager."

Note: A **packager** is a separate company that performs all the operations that publishers used to perform, such as developing manuscripts, copyediting them, setting the type, selecting and producing the art package, proofreading, indexing, and sometimes marketing. Packagers are often former employees of publishing houses, sometimes they are subsidiaries of composition (typesetting) firms, or they might be sole proprietorships freelancing everything from a home office. The publisher pays the packager; often the packager (not the publisher) pays the freelancer. Sometimes the freelancer has to wait until the publisher pays the packager before he or she is paid. Like any other entity, some are good, some not so good.

A **production editor**, **production manager**, or **director of production** is responsible for buying all the services and materials necessary for publishing the book, and for keeping the production process within budget and on schedule. The **production team** consists of many people:

The **art director** is responsible for the following:
- Book designers, who prepare sample designs and draw up the specifications for the physical appearance of the product
- Graphic artists, who work on computer or on paper
- Photographers
- Production assistants, who scale photographs and illustrations for production and keep itemized logs of production tasks and pieces

The **editorial manager** or **project editor** is in charge of the following:
- Copyeditors
- Indexers
- Proofreaders
- Permissions clerks
- All editorial components of the manuscript

The **assistant production editor** or **type buyer** is responsible for getting estimates of schedules and costs for the following:
- Compositors (typesetters), which could involve in-house desktop publishing specialists or outside composition companies
- Paper suppliers
- Printers
- Binding suppliers

WHY SCHEDULES ARE IMPORTANT

Schedules help keep all the different teams on track. Not only must the production team make sure the paper arrives at the printer's on schedule so that printing is finished to accommodate the binder's schedule, but all the preceding steps have to be synchronized just to get to that point. In addition to production's concerns are those of the marketing department, which has arranged author interviews and presentations, rented booth space at conferences to introduce the book, and bought advertising so the wholesale distributor can deliver the books and collect the revenue to pay for all of this.

So, if your computer freaks out or your printer dies, as an indexer you are not readjusting a schedule merely with the person on the telephone, but you might be affecting other schedules as well. (Of course, any experienced production or project editor builds in wobble time, but in publishing, wobble time is a hot commodity that evaporates rapidly.)

HOW FREELANCE WORK IS ASSIGNED

Editorial freelancers, including indexers, usually work with project editors. Project editors have lists of freelancers with whom they have previously worked, and they give work preferentially to a freelancer who has produced good indexes on time at a rate within budget. Project editors inherit such lists from former production editors; they add to such lists when information comes across their desks in the form of brochures, inquiry letters (with resumes), referrals from others in the industry, and by word of mouth.

Often, project editors handle 10 or more titles at a time, all in various stages of production. They work with various copyeditors, proofreaders, and indexers simultaneously as well as authors; solve problems that arise with the art components of the manuscript; create and establish style guides for each title; and attend "launch" meetings with the rest of the production team, a marketing representative, the executive editor or the developmental editor, and sometimes the author.

The production editor's desk is a place where Captain Kirk does not ever want to go. It is awash in 15-page launch memos, style sheets, marked copies of proof from authors that must be reviewed and have marks transposed to master sets of proof from proofreaders, Post-It notes, invoices, and a copyedited manuscript from a new freelancer that must be reviewed. Somewhere in the mess is a floppy disk with an index (perhaps under the blueline proofs of the front matter of a book that is weeks behind schedule). And, in this pile is the log where all of these comings and goings of paper need to be recorded, lest the final pages for an author's professional memoir get mixed up with those for the textbook of prostate surgery.

Do not presume that anyone in the publishing house has any reason to be more organized than Noah trying to feed and clean up after all the animals while dealing with seasickness. Remember, even though you specifically might be a whiz with computers, many authors, editors, and publishing executives are still making a transition from paper-based information to electronically transmitted information. Lots of people still working out there loathe computers or think of them only as high-tech typewriters.

You, as a freelancer new to the field, called this project editor two weeks ago, and have not heard anything since. You wonder, should I call again?

Possible scenarios:
- Voicemail takes your message and deletes it.
- The project editor answers the phone, tells you he or she is interested, and never gets back to you because a major crisis has just hatched on the desk.
- The project editor actually records your name and phone number and puts it on the "possibles" list.
- You have called when the project editor has all the usual indexers tied up with other projects or received rejections, has a book schedule going into meltdown, and needs an indexer now.

BATTLEFIELD COMMISSIONS, OR HOW TO GET NOTICED IN THE CHAOS

Because project editors juggle so many projects at a time, yet remain accountable for editorial quality control, they tend to choose the most experienced or most referred freelancers first. Taking on a new freelancer, no matter how extensive the resume or the referral, always poses a time commitment to project editors, who must instruct the new worker on house style or specifications as well as the needs of the specific book and then must review the finished work either in-progress or upon submission. Time being the editor's least renewable resource, consider what you would do in a similar situation. Unless you call at the moment the editor panics about a project, most likely your name will not stand out.

Nonetheless, prepare a professional resume and business cards (office discount store paper stock suffices), and contact those project editors. Your resume will provide a physical presence for you that the editor can file.

Getting the details correct is important. If the information on your cover letter is wrong, you are announcing to a prospective employer that you do not spend time on details, which gets your paperwork immediately trashed.

Whether you send your papers first or call first, make a follow-up call one or two weeks after sending off your packet of information. Make a polite inquiry, short and concise, stressing that you have time available in your schedule. Be prepared to quote or estimate approximate fees, but give such information on a contingency basis because you have not seen any job yet and you have no experience with this editor. If the discussion has gotten this far, you might also inquire about the publisher's standard pay scale.

Continue to make similar follow-ups every six to eight weeks; send holiday cards too. Project editors get lots of inquiries about freelance work, and keeping your name in their memory banks is important. This is reinforced if they also see your name in freelance industry lists, like *Indexer Locator* produced by the ASI or in *Literary Market Place*. But, above all, don't make yourself a pest or whine—know when to back off. If an editor decides to hire a new freelancer, the next most "professional" candidate is considered first.

THINK TIMELINES

What is the production cycle like for specific publishers? Elementary/high school (elhi) publishers must have copies of their textbooks on teacher's or district supervisor's desks no later than March for fall adoptions; that puts busy times around the previous November running into December. When does COMDEX occur for computer books? Or MacWorld? When is the next convention of the Radiological Society of North America (the largest health-affiliated convention)? Convention costs are high, and publishers need the books on hand to sell them. Hobby, art, and special interest books like biographies must hit the stores for Christmas at least by Thanksgiving. Figure no less than two months for printing and binding, and indexes slip in right before that, so calculate the best times to target specific project editors.

WHAT ABOUT CONTRACTS?

Many project editors rely only on verbal agreements regarding dates due for completed work, fees, and promised receipt of page proofs. More and more, however, send purchase orders with the proofs, and these orders or the PO number must accompany your invoice or you will not receive payment. Reasonable business practice recommends that the freelancer prepare a letter of agreement sent to the project editor as soon as possible following the assignment. You may request that the project editor or production manager sign or initial the agreement and return a copy to you, especially if this is the first time you have worked with this editor or publisher. At a minimum, this provides both parties an opportunity to review the facts of the agreement and to adjust it if necessary; at worst, you have a document that might give you a legal edge in nonpayment claims.

Some publishers have formal contracts created by their legal departments, most of which include copyright transferal or work-for-hire clauses. Some indexers provide their own contracts, but understand that the project editor probably does not have the authority to sign a formal contract without submitting it to corporate counsel for approval, which may delay the assignment and gives the project editor one more item to log and track. (As a business owner, a freelancer who has penned a contract should probably have it reviewed by a lawyer to guarantee its legality.)

Regarding the prospect of nonpayment, some indexers include a statement in a letter of agreement or on the invoice that payment is due in 30 days, and copyright for the index is released to the publisher only upon full payment. This sounds like a good idea to me.

HOW DO I FORMAT THE INDEX?

First, ask the project editor. Some publishing houses have strict format guidelines; many do not. The editor will send guidelines if necessary. If doubt exists, send the editor a sample.

DO I COMMUNICATE WITH THE AUTHOR?

Ask the project editor. Some publishers actively promote such communication; others discourage it. Some authors do not understand the art of professional indexing and interfere with the process rather than assist it. Others can give freelancers a perspective on the subject of the book and clarify terminology. Never contact an author unless the project editor has approved or requested the contact, and never ever comment on the production job itself or publication dates; refer the author to the project editor or the publisher.

Sometimes an editor or author requests a sample of the index in progress to review content or format along the way. Always make certain he or she is aware that what you are sending is incomplete and only a draft copy.

Note: I try to send about two chapters from the middle of the book. I usually do not index the first chapter of most books first because the first three chapters or so are often theoretical or introductory and do not represent the greater part of the text. For that reason, they are also the most difficult to index. However, I usually read them first for their introductory perspective.

WHAT GOES ON THE INVOICE?

The invoice must contain your essential information, your Social Security number, any purchase order (PO) number, the date, the authors' last names, the book title, and the edition. If you know it, include the International Standard Book Number (ISBN) of the title. I include the fee formula (n pages @ $N; n lines @ $N), the return postage, and the total. An invoice cannot be processed without a Social Security, tax identification, or employee identification number. Keep a copy for your records. Before you return or discard the proof, take a copy of the title page and copyright page if you have them and keep them for future reference as well.

DID THEY LIKE IT?

Always follow-up in some manner with a new client. Sometimes a project editor does not have time to do a thorough review or just sends a copy to the author for review. Sometimes (alas!), the index is commissioned by a production assistant who knows little about editorial or indexing standards and is wholly incapable of giving feedback. More often than not, you only get "We didn't hear any complaints."

So, maybe that and payment in 30 days is enough after all.

Chapter 4

Independent Contractor Status: The Indexer's Role

Kate Mertes © 2001

Indexers who perform freelance work are sometimes asked to provide "proof" of their independent status. Clients who ask for this type of information are usually trying to protect themselves from investigation or suits by the IRS or the United States Department of Labor (DOL) because, though employers must withhold federal and state employment taxes from their employees' wages, freelance workers are responsible for paying their own taxes. In addition, independent contractor status relieves clients from a number of other employment burdens, such as providing employee benefits, payment of unemployment insurance taxes and workers' compensation premiums, some overtime and minimum wage requirements, and liability under many employment discrimination laws, such as Title VII of the Civil Rights Act of 1964 and the Age Discrimination in Employment Act (ADEA).

The information requested by clients may represent an intrusion into an indexers' privacy. Publishers have been known to ask for copies of indexer tax returns, contracts and invoices for other clients, client lists, etc., information to which clients have no real legal right and which might be used in ways that are harmful to the indexer. One colleague on the ASI listserv (ASI-L) recently reported that, when the indexer provided copies of client invoices, the publisher lowered her payment to the per-page price charged to the other client!

Although corporate lawyers are often behind a client's attempts to collect this material, such information is in fact fairly useless to the client. That's because, in independent contractor/employee status investigations, the investigating agency is not necessarily focusing on the freelancer, or any of the freelancer's other clients; it's checking out the specific relationship between the client and the freelancer. An indexer might very well have an employment relationship with one client and a freelance relationship with another. This basic fact cannot be stressed enough: It's not your status that's in question, it's the nature of the relationship between you and your client; it's the client who is being investigated, not you.

Remembering this key issue will make it much easier for you to deal with a publisher who requests proof of your independent contractor status. You don't have a status to prove, except in relationship to each individual client.

WHAT'S IN A NAME?

"Freelancer," "independent contractor," and "contingent worker" are phrases you may hear bandied about. Freelancers and independent contractors are essentially the same thing: workers who contract with a client to do a specific job, rather than engaging in continuous employment under the control of the employer. The phrase "contingent worker," a real buzzword at the moment, refers to a much broader range of non-full-time workers, including part-time and temporary employees and independent contractors. So, just because your client considers you a contingent worker, it doesn't necessarily mean that you are not an employee. These terms are important because the IRS will be looking at the language you and your client use to describe your relationship.

However, just because contracts, letters of agreement, and other documents refer to you as an independent contractor rather than an employee, it doesn't mean that's what you are in the eyes of the IRS. Terminology is important in worker classification, but the actual relationship is what investigators will be examining. Specifically, they'll want to determine how much control the client exerts over the worker.

CONTROL AND EMPLOYMENT STATUS

Federal employment and tax laws use a number of different tests to determine the nature of the relationship between you and your client. These tests are often somewhat subjective and seldom involve either-or questions but look at the degree and extent of significant elements. The most frequently used concept comes from common law and is often known as the right-to-control test. An employment relationship is considered to exist if the client has the right to control and direct the worker. Note that it is the right to control, rather than the actual exercise of that control, which is the critical factor. The concept of control is central to most methods of determining the nature of the relationship between client and worker.

The DOL uses the economic reality test to classify an employer's workers. This test involves five factors:

1. Are the services provided by the worker integral to the employer's business? To what extent?
2. How permanent is the relationship between client and worker?
3. Is the worker investing in facilities and equipment, or are they chiefly provided by the client?
4. Does the worker have an independent hand in the amount of profit or loss he or she makes?
5. How much initiative, judgment, or foresight must the worker rely on in serving the client?

Once again, these are not cut-and-dried rules. Many independent contractors work in their clients' facilities or are provided software by their clients, without being regarded as employees. It's a matter of the extent to which the contractor is under the control of the client that determines the existence of an employment relationship.

The IRS has developed a 20-step test to determine worker classification; over time the relevance of the various factors has mutated, and auditors seldom work their way through the entire process. Instead, they look at behavioral factors:

- Can the client set the hours of work?
- Is the worker expected to work on a full-time basis for the client?
- Does the contract require the personal services of the worker?
- Is the relationship between worker and client continuing and indefinite, or closely defined by the boundaries of individual projects?
- Can the client require the worker to follow instructions as to when, where, or how to work (as opposed to setting requirements for the end result of the project)?

IRS auditors also look at financial controls:

- Does the contractor hire and supervise his or her own assistants, or is the client in control of them?
- Is payment made by the hour, week, or month, rather than for specific work performed?
- Is the worker bearing the main burden of investment in facilities and equipment, or is the client heavily underwriting costs?

In addition, the IRS also looks at how the client and the worker perceive their relationship:

- Are termination or discharge rights written into the contract?
- Do the workers make their services available to the general public?
- Does the contractor undertake to provide services for other clients?

Note that, in all instances, the central issue is really one of control. How much say does the client have over when, how, and where the worker does a job? Fuller descriptions of the IRS and DOL regulations for determining worker classification are available in a number of human resource law publications, including works published by the Bureau of National Affairs, Commerce Clearinghouse, and Thompson Publishing Group, both in print and online; or, one can consult the regulations themselves by checking out published regulations for the agencies in most local libraries or via their government Web sites (www.irs.gov, and www.dol.gov). But remember that, while understanding the independent contractor classification rules is useful, the worker is under no obligation to prove his or her status. The onus is on the client to prove the lack of an employment relationship to the government.

A MATTER OF DEGREE

Reading through the factors involved in employment relationship tests may cause alarm bells to go off in the heads of freelancers. After all, some of the enumerated characteristics of an employee seem to fit some freelancers. Many freelancers work by the hour, for instance. Some freelancers may only work for one client. And surely most clients exercise considerable control over the outcome of the work—they are paying for a specific sort of project, after all.

The presence or absence of no one specific factor determines the existence of an employment relationship. A judgment call on the worker's status vis-à-vis the client is a matter of degree and extent of control, and lawsuits often hinge on subjective interpretations of the facts. Payment by the hour is probably most significant in the presence of other client requirements like set hours, a full-time commitment, or an indefinite period of work for the client. While one of the factors in both the DOL and the IRS regulations is evidence of the freelancer working for other people, it's more the availability of the freelancer to advertise his or her services to the general public rather than the actual taking on of other clients; one can be an independent contractor and still work entirely or mostly for a single client.

Of course, clients usually have a great deal to say over the format and quality of the final outcome. They are paying for it, after all. Control over the product is quite different from control over the process, however. For instance, the client's specifications regarding the final index—that it be provided in Microsoft Word format, that it contain specific codes for each field, that it be in run-in form, that its quality be of a certain standard—are all control over the final product. But if the client requires you to work on nothing but its product for a specific time period expects, you to work from 9-to-5 and to be available by telephone or e-mail during that time period, calculates your pay for a time period rather than for the project, and requires you to use a specific index-dedicated software even though the final product is to be delivered as a Rich Text Format (RTF) file, that's control over the process, and is a red flag for an employment relationship.

PROTECTING THE WORKER

So what does one do when a client requests inappropriate or highly personal information in order to have evidence of your independent contractor status? Clients sometimes act as if the worker classification rules were written for their benefit, but that's not the case. The IRS and DOL regulations are meant to protect the government first (because an employer pays a great deal more in employment taxes for each employee than self-employed persons pay for themselves), and to protect workers second, who when classified as independent contractors are not eligible for many valuable employee benefits and are not protected under a number of antidiscrimination laws.

The recent case of *Vizcaino vs. Microsoft Corp.* (aspects of which are still wending their way through the courts) illustrates the protective purpose of employment relationship tests. A group of Microsoft contractors brought in under working conditions very similar to those of Microsoft employees sued the company over their entitlement to retirement and stock purchase plan benefits. As a result, these workers were reclassified as employees and Microsoft ended up paying heavy penalties and back taxes, as well as being required to provide employment benefits for the reclassified workers.

The *Vizcaino* case has alarmed many companies who regularly use independent contractors, and the case probably accounts for the recent rise in corporate attempts to gather information from freelancers. But the wise freelancer will keep in mind that it is the client, not the worker, who is liable for penalties and back taxes should the investigating agency decide an employment relationship does indeed exist. Being aware of the purpose and interpretation of the relevant laws and regulations can help freelancers decide what to provide to clients and will also give the smart independent contractor the nerve required to make clear to clients the inappropriate nature of some of their information requests.

These two points can't be stressed enough:
1. The client is the one who has to prove something, not you.
2. The point in question is not the worker's status in itself but the relationship between the worker and the client.

Don't give anything to the client that doesn't deal with that relationship in some way. Requests for information from clients may seem hard to refuse. One doesn't wish to alienate a potential source of income. But do be prepared to negotiate what sort of information you turn over. The client doesn't need your tax forms (be assured that the IRS can certainly get those on its own, if necessary). The client has no business getting a list of names and addresses of other parties you have worked for, and certainly has no right to see invoices you've submitted to other clients. If the client wants evidence that the contractor is available to offer his or her services to the general public, a business card and a curriculum vitae (especially if it lists recent jobs for other clients), copies of advertisements or flyers, or listings in professional directories (such as the *Indexer Locator*) are quite sufficient to prove that fact.

Investigators will be most interested in the terms of the contract(s) between the worker and the client under investigation. Feel free to point this out to your client when negotiating those terms. Contractors who understand the control issue and its relevant indicators can use that understanding to bargain their way to a better contract.

TAKING ADVANTAGE OF INDEPENDENT CONTRACTOR STATUS

Most large companies who use lots of freelancers have standard contracts and rates. In most cases, these are not negotiable; in fact, they also tend to be the fairest contracts available, having been vetted by experienced lawyers and proven effective over time. But if the terms of a contract are negotiable, the client's interest in ensuring that the employment relationship devil doesn't raise its ugly head can be used to get the terms the freelancer wants.

Indexers who are fast workers often feel that hourly payment rates penalize them for being efficient. If the terms of the contract are negotiable, don't hesitate to point out that the IRS and DOL regulations specifically state that payment by the hour is one factor in determining the right to control. Many indexers have had the unfortunate experience of taking on jobs for extremely anxious authors, who constantly want to check entries and get progress reports or want the indexer to work on nothing but their book until it is done. In such situations, gently point out that if one acquiesces to these terms, the author would be an employer and would have to pay employment taxes. Send them to the relevant government sites to check the independent contractor versus employee regulations. They will often leave you alone to get the work done after that.

While we all are happy to turn in progress reports and sometimes in-progress indexes on long jobs, many indexers balk at doing so unless there is some sort of payment/deliverables exchange. If you'd like to get the author or editor off your back, point out that midstream vetting of work could be construed as indicative of an employment relationship. The same thing goes for those pesky subject lists sometimes foisted on indexers by overeager authors. They can be helpful, but if author recommendations are becoming a nuisance, raise the control issue.

Freelance indexers don't have to understand the worker classification rules, but it certainly helps when it comes to dealing with client requests for information and negotiating contract terms.

This chapter previously appeared in Key Words, *Vol. 8, Issue 2, March/April 2000.*

Chapter 5

Setting Fees

Jan C. Wright © 2001

Professional indexing has gotten a lot more complex these days, especially when it comes to figuring out a fee for a project. It used to be that you could set fees fairly easily after seeing pages from a proposed book. You would look at the size of the page, the density of the material, the number of entries you thought would be generated, and make your bid.

But now, pages may not even exist in the text you are indexing. You may be presented with Web pages, topics in an online help system, material for a CD-ROM, or even material that will be used in three different ways. An example of this multi-use material would be a book that will be printed, but whose files will also be copied onto a CD-ROM, and run through a macro to create Web pages. How do you charge for all these varied indexing situations?

I, for one, have never been into the complex process of figuring out my per-page fees, converting them to an hourly rate, and worrying about how much I am making that way. I have seen messages on the ASI listserv (ASI-L) that tell you how to do the calculations, but I try to keep things much simpler. I set fees by the difficulty of the project *for me* and the amount of technical knowledge it requires to produce the index.

PER-PAGE RATES

If a piece is going to be sent to me as ready-to-go pages, with page numbers assigned, I will do a per-page fee. Set rates like that are only good for set pages; in other words, keep thinking "How easy will this be for me to do? Pages already printed, unlikely to change much? Okay, set fee is fine then." I don't use per-line or per-entry fees and have never run into a publisher who wished me to work that way. I think it would change how I index if I did! Per-page fees these days run anywhere from $3.00 per page to $7.00 for highly technical material.

Example: 350-page book @ 3.50 per page = $1225

If you decide to use per-line or per-entry fees, make sure you discuss with the client what an entry is and what a line is. To me, it seems to change every time people talk about it. For instance, is the following three entries or four?

>   Dogs. See also Mammals
>   big dogs, 42
>   small dogs, 47, 58

The confusion doesn't keep things clear and simple, and there is room for argument, so I avoid it.

Being clear about what you are charging for also matters in a per-page rate. Do you charge for long pages of technical code, pages containing only pictures, blank pages, tables of contents, glossaries? I follow Lynn Moncreif's rule of thumb: If I have to think about whether it needs to be indexed, I charge for it. Tables of contents are automatically out, and so are blank pages for me (although I know of some folks who do charge for them). I charge for pages of code or pictures, but not for glossaries if I am not indexing them. I charge full rate for half pages, or pages with just a little text on them, figuring other pages in the book make up for them.

I'm also unusual in that I charge a whole lot less for small presses (I call it my "small press fee" since I know they can't afford much and since their books are usually really fun.) I take fees from a small press that I wouldn't ever consider taking from a larger company. These pieces are usually neither technical nor deep, are already prepared, and don't require me to use anything other than my indexing software package.

Requesting sample pages before bidding is essential. Even after years of working as an indexer, if I get sloppy and don't ask, I can wind up in trouble. Every indexer indexes at a different rate, so you can figure out on your own how long a project will take, and therefore how much per hour you make. But I look at per-page projects almost as a vacation. They are so easy to do, and I don't have to track my hours unless I really want.

If you must send the index by Federal Express or Express Mail to your clients, they should pay for that service. Try to get that charge agreed to up front. I usually e-mail everything these days, so that does not come up very often.

HOURLY RATES

For all other projects, I use either an hourly fee, or a combination of per-page and hourly. Let's talk about hourly first.

I charge hourly fees for projects where the text is going to be changing while I am working on it and for anything involving embedded indexing or online work. The reasoning is that I will most likely be putting in more than one pass on materials, troubleshooting why the index won't compile, helping to design the index interface and behavior, downloading and tracking live copies of files, resolving issues about getting the index codes to work with the software, and most important, providing at my own expense a lot of different expensive software packages to comply with my clients' needs. Keeping things like FrameMaker, RoboHelp, Word, PageMaker, Excel, and Web software current is expensive.

Another reason that hourly works better in these electronic file situations is that even with a simple Word file, determining how many pages are in the file depends on the machine you are using. Word files grow and shrink depending on the targeted printer, and your printer will not be the same as the client's. One indexer complained on the listserv about the client's estimate of pages and how the client was being shortchanged on a per-page fee. The client said the file was only x number pages, which it was on his printer. On the indexer's printer, however, the file rolled out to x + 5 pages. So, per-page rates are not a great idea with electronic files.

Note: Portable Document Format (PDF) files, however, do not do this rolling behavior. Being stable, they are a good substitute for printed galleys, and you can do a per-page rate on them.

Often a client will want to put a cap on the number of hours for a project. One of the hardest things in online work is figuring out how long it will take to do a project, with lots of unknowns. Each and every project varies so much in its demands, whether it will go smoothly, whether there will be rework, whether the client has figured out how to display the index or not, how much interaction you have with programmers, whether you are expected to incorporate review comments into the index, etc. All you can do is estimate from some sample topics, ask for lots of samples, and set up a very clear process with the client that outlines your exact responsibility. An average estimate can be 40 to 50 topics in eight hours, adding on time for editing and troubleshooting.

Example:
347-topic help file @ $40 per hour x 60 hours = $2400

Lately, I have seen an alarming trend in embedded indexing—publishers offering per-page rates and wanting the embedded work done for that rate as well as index development. Keep in mind these are two difficult and skilled tasks the publisher is asking you to do. Not only must you develop a good index, but you must also know the embedded software, pay for it, and keep its constraints in mind while you are developing the index for it. Part of what the publisher needs to pay for is your technical skill in the software package—you must *know* that package inside and out. PageMaker, for instance, has a 50-character per level limit—that means that your main heading can only be 50 characters long, and all subheads can only be 50 characters long. Try writing an index sometime with lots of State Department names in it for a PageMaker index; it can be horrifying!

Embedding is twice as much work as simply developing an index. Those of us who have done it a long time have some tricks for making it easier and faster, but it is still extra work on your part with extra costs to support the software and hardware requirements. You usually must advise the client on such matters as what the software can and can't do, how files must be set up to work correctly, and how to treat the files after they have been indexed. A per-page rate, and low rates like the ones I have seen offered, just do not cover your costs. Don't take these low-paying jobs if you don't have to! We need to train these publishers to see how complex the work we do is, and to pay for it.

COMBINATION RATES

If the author of a printed piece is making changes, and I have to go over a book and find all the changes and update the index, I may charge a combination rate—per page for the initial index development and then hourly for the changes. This combination rate also works well for embedded work; you can charge a per-page fee for development of the index and then hourly for the embedded work itself. This only works if you develop the index outside of the program and do all your embedding in one fell swoop. Otherwise, separating out the tasks of development and embedding is too confusing.

Example:
350-page book @ 3.50 per page for development	$1225
25 hours embedding into PageMaker @ $40 per hour	$1000
Total:	$2225

INVOICING

Make sure your invoice clearly states what the title of the project was, the name of your contact at the company, and clear terms of payment. I also include my Employer Identification Number (EIN), which is like a Social Security number for corporations (the client has to have it at tax time). If you are not incorporated, put your social security number on the invoice. Clients will probably call you anyway at tax time to get that number, but if they are on the ball, they may remember to get it from your invoice. If you feel wary of putting the number on your invoice, don't, but be ready to get a lot of phone calls in January asking for it.

Clear terms of payment, and any penalties for overdue payments, should be spelled out. But no matter what you put down as payment terms, don't expect payment before 30 days. Most companies simply cannot do that with their accounting systems, no matter how we feel about it as small business owners. The usual path through a company's accounting system is complex, and it usually runs checks only at specific times, like once a week or once a month. Getting a check run especially for you is not usually an option. If you just consider 30 days as usual, and budget yourself accordingly, you won't have many surprises. Early checks are always a delight!

KEEPING THINGS SIMPLE

Keep things as simple as you can with your rate schedules. Decide what the lowest rate is that you will accept for certain work and keep track of your projects for hourly rate estimates so that you get better at predicting them.

With all the varying rates and ways of charging, be sure to note down what you quoted to a client. Keep the e-mail, or make a note on the project's folder, or record that information somewhere. It's guaranteed that you will forget what you said by the time the project arrives, or by the time the project is finished. Unless, of course, it is a beastly project, and the only way you can finish it is to tell yourself over and over again how much money you are making on it.

Chapter 6

Charging by the Entry
Nan Badgett © 2001

Less common than charging per indexable page is charging per index entry. According to the ASI 2000 Salary Survey, only 25 percent of indexers surveyed charge by the entry. However, in certain subject areas such as medical and scientific indexing, this method is often the payment method of choice since it compensates the indexer for the extremely detailed work required in these fields. Charging by the entry may also be preferred in periodical or database indexing where a consistent number of entries per publication or issue are generated.

The biggest question raised by this method is the definition of an entry. The answer varies from any concept, regardless of heading level, with at least one locator or cross-reference, to each page reference. With this discrepancy in answers, the problem in counting entries is obvious. If each concept is counted in (in the example below), the indexer could charge for four entries. If each page reference is counted, the number of entries doubles.

Example:

    hepatitis
        types, 30-32, 41-43
        causes, 33-38
        risk factors, 44-47, 128
        treatments, 100-105, 228-230, 321-323

The key then is that the indexer and client agree upon the definition of an entry. And of course there is the task of counting entries. While indexing software may be used to count entries, one has to be sure that the software is using the same counting method agreed upon with the client.

Another point of agreement with the client should be the average number of entries per page. This figure reflects the depth of indexing and actual amount of work involved in producing the index and prevents the indexer from padding entries. From this point of view, charging by the entry appears more accurate than charging by the page. If it is more accurate, is it more lucrative?

An indexer who charges $0.60 per entry and is expected to generate an average of five entries per page is working at the equivalent of $3 per indexable page. This may not seem so lucrative when other indexers working for $3 per page might be expected to generate only two or three entries per page. In very dense material such as medical books, however, the per entry rate protects the indexer. For example, if an indexer is expected to generate eight entries per page, the $0.60 per entry fee reflects a per page rate of $4.80 per page. Few if any publishers would pay that for a lightly indexed trade book. Clearly, the more important figure is how well the indexer is being compensated when the per-entry rate (or per-page rate) is translated to a per hour rate.

In May of 2000, charges per entry ranged from $0.15 to $1.10, while hourly rates ranged from $15 to $60.

Chapter 7

Educating Publishers (or How to Deal with Low-Paying Clients)

Maria Coughlin © 2001

What is the content of the publication to be indexed at $2/page? How long is the publication? I have done, and still do, work for that rate when the content is ridiculously easy to enter. I can do up to 45 pages in an hour and not cry myself to sleep. Also, ridiculously easy and fast indexes can be turned around in three to five days.

I find it very difficult to make any judgments about rates and turnaround times until I've discussed the project in detail with the publisher's agent, be it editor, production house, or (sometimes) compositor. As a businessperson, I try to remember that the customer/client is always absolutely right, even when he or she needs some gentle guidance away from the edge of a cliff. Which is my way of saying I'm never insulted when someone offers me work, and I can almost always educate the customer/client about equitable payment if I use patience and tact. In addition, I have been known to discount (decrease) an already agreed-upon rate (horrors!) when I think the client may be paying way too much for a job. I prefer to keep my clients happy and reassured about my professionalism and honesty. In the long run, they turn out to be loyal and appreciative people who will cooperate with me (for example, by giving me an extended deadline when calamity strikes).

I've also bundled jobs before. I'll take on a low-paying job if the publisher agrees to send me four or five more reasonably priced jobs within the following year. It doesn't hurt to take a long-term average view of the bottom line. As bean counters have taken over in publishing, publishers have had to take the same long-term average approach.

If I have to turn down a job, I say "I'm sorry I can't fit that into my schedule right now; it would be irresponsible of me to try when my schedule's so full already. Please keep me in mind for future indexes because I'd like an opportunity to demonstrate to you that I can produce high-quality indexes on time."

Finally, at Editorial Services, I don't allow my associate indexers to present me with a problem unless they can also present me with a proposed solution. This cuts down on the number of problems I'm presented with. If an associates cogitates on a proposed solution, he or she can often find a working solution, and it makes me look good when I say, "Yes, kid, you're on the right track! Pull up a chair and let's get this sorted out." It doesn't hurt to approach one's client the same way: "I'd love to index *How Chocolate Enhances Your Sex Life and Retards Aging*, but I have a problem with the proposed rate of payment. After examining your sample pages, I've determined that a more equitable rate would be $X per page since the index will require many more (or far fewer) entries per page than I first thought. Long experience has taught me that both of us are better served if we have a clear idea of a fair price for a high-quality index. When this book goes into subsequent editions, as it undoubtedly will, it would be unfortunate if it became apparent, as it inevitably would, that the original index was unfairly priced. And it will be helpful if, as similar projects land on your desk in future, you're able to forecast accurately what the index will cost."

This approach turns a potential client into a colleague. I'm NEVER concerned that they don't regard me as a professional; I know I'm a professional indexer, and that knowledge is so fundamental to my approach to clients that no cracks have appeared in the foundation yet, no matter what rate or schedule I'm offered. You'll be reading more about this in my forthcoming book, *Publishers Are From Mars, Indexers Are From Jupiter*.

A discussion on the ASI listserv ASI-L, which focused on how to deal with low-paying clients, led to this chapter, reprinted from Key Words *Vol. 8, Issue 2, March/April 2000.*

Chapter 8

Office Space—Four Varieties

Margie Towery © 2001

Four working indexers (Joanne Clendenen, Alexandra Nickerson, Marilyn Rowland, and Richard Shrout) were asked to describe their office space and how it is organized.

JOANNE CLENDENEN

I work inside my home, partly because I have a good amount of space, and partly because it allows me to be here for the comings and goings of my school-age children. After seeing my friends deal with the hassles of renting office space, I'm glad I'm at home.

I have the good fortune of having a large house with a so-called game room that I have converted into my office. The only things it lacks are full enclosure with a door and enough file cabinets. I live in Houston, so there isn't much to look at outside the windows, trust me. I have the two windows of the room on my right as I work, which give me light but not glare. I work in an L-shaped configuration, with an old desk facing the windows and my workstation facing the wall to the left of the desk.

I think my workstation is the most interesting part of my layout because I didn't opt for one of those ready-made things with the shelves and all. I find that they don't have enough horizontal workspace. Instead, I have a door—a solid wooden door—laid atop two sawhorses (soon, I hope, to be replaced by two two-drawer file cabinets). It's a nice wide door and makes a great, deep workspace. I have my monitor directly in front of me on the table/door, with the computer to the right and the printer on top of it. My document stand sits to the left of the monitor, and I still have room for an accordion tickle file folder and phone on the far left. My in-baskets and such are on the old desk. I use a standard office chair with wheels that allows me to shift orientation from table to desk. My bookcase with references is to my left as I face the computer, so I can swing over there, too.

I'm still working on lighting. I have two standard lamps, one on the desk and one to my left to illuminate my document stand, but I really need some overhead track lighting.

For reading and marking, I have an old upholstered rocking chair, not ideal, but fairly comfortable, when I can get a turn using it. It's often occupied by my feline office assistant.

ALEXANDRA NICKERSON

Organization? Probably the most significant factor in the organization of my office is the office itself. For reasons unrelated to organization, I moved my office out of my home more than 10 years ago. This move, to a nearby rented 9 x 12-foot office, soon proved to have many hidden benefits. No longer did I worry when a chapter turned up missing that I had mixed it in with the newspapers to be recycled. All my indexing materials arrived at the office and no other materials did, so it was easy to keep track of my projects. No longer was my work spread between my desk and the other spots in the house where I'd settled in to mark, proof, or edit a printout. The arrival of houseguests no longer meant putting away the current project. Since that move, my office space has grown in several steps and currently occupies a 1,000-square-foot condominium I purchased when I discovered that my monthly mortgage payments would be less than the rental I was paying on my last office.

Because I work on multiple projects simultaneously, I needed a system to keep the materials for each together. I use a basket system purchased from one of the home improvement store chains for this purpose. Each project has its own 15 x 20-inch wire mesh basket (or several, for large projects, where all proof is placed once it is logged and checked for missing pages. Clear plastic sleeves holding a tag with the name of the project identify each basket, which can be removed like a drawer from the stack and carried to the work surface when I want to work on that project. The basket system itself occupies one side of a closet in the room I use for copying, shipping, and storage. A second, smaller stack of baskets holds shipping materials sorted by carrier so that they are easy to find when the pickup cutoff is only minutes away.

The middle room of my condo contains a large corner that provides plenty of workspace for marking up proof as well as bill paying, correspondence, and the like. Near the sliding glass door is my computer desk, one of those modular desks with a separate set of drawers that rolls underneath on wheels. At the left there is a return that can also roll under the desk, which provides plenty of landing space for proof as I work. At the right is a bookcase with reference books I most often consult (for many issues I find books faster and easier than interrupting myself to log on to the Internet). From my position at the computer, I can look out at the woods behind the condo, where I often see deer as well as birds, chipmunks, and squirrels. Indoor companionship is provided by a pair of zebra finches (Watch out—they are the rabbits of the avian world!)

The third room of the condo tends to acquire the overflow of things I don't have time to deal with at the moment, in order to keep the clutter out of sight. For me, as for many of my fellow indexers, clutter creates a sense of pressure that interferes with my ability to work efficiently. When I don't have time to eliminate the clutter, putting it out of sight helps me maintain my focus on my work until I have time to handle it.

MARILYN ROWLAND

My office is full of wonderful things: my computer, laser printer, stand-alone fax machine, telephones, CD player/cassette player/radio, and television set/VCR combinations (initially justified because I wanted to watch some software instruction videos), and an as yet uninstalled scanner. There are books, papers, stacks of page proofs that have already been indexed, and stacks of page proofs that I have yet to index. I have four tables, laid out in a U-shape to accommodate this richness. A dog or cat is usually under the table to keep my feet warm. Several built-in and freestanding bookcases line the walls. The rest of the wall space is taken up by textile arts and pottery, wooden objects, and enamel-on-copper artwork from Chile, Guatemala, Peru, Ecuador, and Panama, and a few of my own efforts at creating artwork.

My office stretches beyond these four walls, though. Just outside my office is another room, the so-called homework room, which doubles as a guestroom. This room also contains a computer and printer, a table, and a desk. Here my kids can do their homework and search the Web. Here, too, I am teaching my husband how to index, and I am beginning to move my Web page design work here because the kids' computer is a newer one than mine. And there is, at the moment at least, more free space in the homework room. In the living room, I keep my newly purchased photocopy machine. (Doesn't everyone?) I need to reorganize my office a bit before I can find space for it there.

In my office, I sit between two windows and can easily look beyond my computer screen to the world outside. But I usually don't, unless the dog is barking and I need to check on which overnight delivery service is at the door. I am usually too absorbed by the world within my computer screen (a challenging index, an inexplicable Web site design problem, or an e-mail from a client or friend) and the world immediately surrounding it. Besides the work-related items are far too many arts and crafts supplies, which enable me, in those rare periods without deadlines, to engage in all sorts of distracting but creative endeavors.

Every once in a while, I think briefly about someday returning to work in a "real" office, but I really don't want to leave my home office!

RICHARD SHROUT

My office is found in a distant corner of the basement where only a single shaft of light can penetrate, which is actually okay because most of my indexing work is really done by moonlight. My office does not pass the IRS test for a home office deduction because it is not used exclusively for business purposes. My wife and daughter both use the Pentium computer attached to a color printer and scanner. Another computer is reserved for my exclusive use only. At least there is a sign on it: "This computer is for Dad's business." It has a laser printer attached to it. I recently purchased a third computer, and I'm in the process of networking all three machines.

Physically they are networked, but the software isn't set up quite correctly yet. During the two or three days that the networking was working correctly, I was able to see the value of it. I could print to either printer from all three machines. I could work on a file on any machine or copy that file to either of the other two.

Redundancy is important to me. I want to prevent being in the position of having to call an editor with the news that a problem on my end will blow the deadline. Given the deadline-intensive nature of indexing, I have built in redundancy to my office wherever possible. Weren't those last two sentences redundant?

(I have already mentioned three computers. I confess there is also a laptop upstairs. Yes, four is overkill, but having at least two machines is a really good idea.)

Something else that has shaped my office is that I am not, repeat not, a neat and tidy person. So I need space to spread out what I am working on. There are two eight-foot tables in this office. Both will hold a very heavy load. I also have two other smaller tables and another 10-foot section of file cabinets with a heavy kitchen counter board across the top. I also have shelves on every wall and a heavy set of metal shelves for books sent to me by publishers.

Now I am getting to the really interesting part. I recently made some new additions to the office and a couple of equally critical deletions. One important addition was a high intensity desk lamp. One side of my office had space for reading but was only lit by fluorescent bulbs—not good. I could not concentrate for very long in that light. The high intensity desk lamp, which is adjustable, throws just the right kind of light. If you do get one, remember they are dangerous because of the heat and should be placed very carefully and turned off when not in use. They are definitely worth the extra effort. To go with the new lamp, I have a little desk table that rolls and a comfortable chair. Also in that area of the office I have the new TV and VCR to add to the CD boombox. Hey, my theory is that if I am going to spend hours down here, there have to be a few things to do for distraction during breaks. I can listen to the TV while I am keying. I mark pages, so keying for me is primarily a data entry chore, which does allow for some distraction for peace of mind.

The most important new addition to the office by far was the new chair for data entry. This chair is wonderful. I won't get into the exact specifics of the chair because each one of us will have our own definition of what makes a wonderful chair. But the method I used to select it is worth passing on. I went to one of the office supply stores which had a large selection of office chairs, and I sat in every chair to find out what was comfortable and what was not. I was amazed to find out that the best chair for me was not the most expensive. The chair I selected is adjustable in height and has good back support.

Let me add here a serious discussion of ergonomics. I found out the hard way a few years ago that repetitive stress syndrome is real and devastating. It can put an indexer out of business. My mistake was to use an eye-level stand for the page that I was reading. I placed the stand to the side of my monitor. It did save neck strain but I was placing great stress on my shoulder taking the pages down from the stand. Suddenly, after indexing a few thousand pages, I was prevented from lifting my arm by a shooting pain in my shoulder which took several months to get over. My solution right now to this page-turning problem is not ideal but it works. I now place the pages to the side of my monitor where I do not have to raise my arm and then place the completed pages on a wooden box beside me. Look for easy, non-stress-inducing motions.

Let me also mention that I use the Microsoft Natural Keyboard for data entry. It works for me. If you have long fingers, meaning you can reach an octave or more on the piano, you will probably like the Natural Keyboard. People with shorter fingers don't usually like it, probably because of the increased distance between many of the keys when compared to a regular keyboard.

One of the reasons that I got the newest computer was to have the PC power available to work with voice recognition software, just to have another way to enter indexes. What would happen if carpal tunnel syndrome did strike or I broke a finger, wrist, or arm? I would just like to spread my redundancy a little wider.

A word about monitors. I have one 17-inch monitor and two 15-inch monitors. Someday, I will purchase a 17-inch monitor for my indexing work, but right now I am satisfied with the 15-inch monitor. Since, I mark proof, my most important work is being done on printouts and not at the computer. If you really do your heavy-duty stuff on the screen, your monitor is then much more critical. I look forward to the flat monitors that most of us will probably be using in the near future.

Since I am a pack rat, not too much goes out or is thrown away. I did figure out early on that the pages have to be thrown out on a regular basis. But I have also been keeping a hard copy of each index. Now that I have a Zip drive for backup, I think that the paper copies will have to go. There is just not enough space. And here's a secret: In 10 years, I have never once referred back to a hard copy of an index. So, perhaps there is a clue here about the need for their retention.

I hope this summary of my inner sanctum secrets has been helpful. It's an arrangement that works for me. Does anyone need a ten-year supply of paper clips? I have a nice metal box full of them.

Portions of this chapter appeared as the column "The ABCs of Indexing—Office Space," in Key Words, *Vol. 7, No.3, May/June 1999.*

Chapter 9

The ABCs of Project Management

Margie Towery © 2001

Three indexers (Anne Leach, Sandi Schroeder, and Barbara Stroup) were asked how they tracked projects. They were asked to describe the steps they move through from the time a client contacts them about a project to its completion.

ANNE LEACH

Most of my clients are long-term friends, so when one calls me with a new job, I know right away all sorts of essentials: what sort of book to expect, how much they'll be paying me, and the arrival and due dates. I record all of that on a tracking sheet I've developed that has spaces for recording all those details, plus the book's length, the editor's name and phone number, and so on. I then keep those tracking sheets in order, by due date of the index, in an in-basket labeled Incoming Jobs. On the same type of tracking sheet, I also remind myself of any time-consuming non-indexing tasks that might interfere with indexing jobs (formerly, a task such as *Key Words*, Jan./Feb. issue would be an example), and I keep these interfiled by date with the indexing jobs. Then, should I get a call and a job offer from a different client, I can easily check due dates in the stack of incoming tasks to see if I can fit another job into my schedule.

Knowing the types of books typical of each client helps me in figuring approximately how many pages per day I'll be able to complete and whether taking on another job is feasible. Of course, it's taken lots of jobs from each client, over the years, to develop a sense of what they typically provide in terms of text density, subject coverage, and level of expertise of the anticipated audience for the book. If the client or the type of book is a new one, I try to get a feel for this sort of information by questioning the client and making copious notes, which I transcribe to one of my worksheets if I get the job.

Another critical piece of the puzzle when trying to decide if I can take on another job—or in deciding how many days in advance of a deadline to begin work on the index—is knowing pretty well my per-day page output for each client's typical book. This is information I've worked out over the years by tracking my page output per hour, using the same tracking sheet. The stack of tracking sheets for upcoming jobs is my control center. It's a type of calendar that I often leaf through to memorize the jobs, their dates, and so on, and to know what to start when. When the pages arrive and I can begin work, I use the "Start," "Stop," and "Cum" columns on the tracking sheet to log in and out for each work session and to record the total number of pages completed and the cumulative pages per hour. This tells me if I'm working enough hours per day to finish in time.

My final use for the tracking sheet comes at the end of the job, when the index is complete and sent off to the client. I tally the total pages of the book, deduct the number of pages I did not have to scan for indexable material (e.g., blank pages, "part art"), and then divide the total pages by the total hours I spent, coming up with a total hourly equivalent rate. (Doing all this on an adding machine with a tape allows me to keep the adding machine tapes.) This becomes my backup for the invoice, which I prepare and mail the same day.

Comparing this to the hourly rate that I believe I have to make in order to survive as a freelancer (and that's a whole 'nother topic) tells me whether I can afford to keep the same per-page rate for that type of book or whether I have to discuss a rate increase or an index density decrease with my client. I then attach the tracking sheet to the back of my copy of the invoice for the job and stack the invoices, by date, oldest on top, in an in-basket labeled "Accounts Receivable." When the check arrives, I attach the stub to the invoice and file it with the tracking sheet in a folder for that client.

Periodically, I leaf through the "receivables" stack to be sure none is getting stale. If one is, I call the client and ask for the check.

Though not very high-tech, this system has worked well for me.

SANDI SCHROEDER

I have found no tracking software that has met my requirements, so I still track on paper and mentally. When I hear from a client, either by phone or e-mail, I try to pin that client down to dates as much as possible. If we are talking about a future project, I ask the client to advise me if the schedule changes. I generally prefer projects to be done as they become available, with the completion dates approximately one week after final proofs are received. This, however, depends on the amount of proof in the final batch.

I work a little differently than some others in that I mark or track my proofs and give them to someone else to do the computer keyboarding and initial cleanup and edit. I then get them back for a final edit. This works well for me, since I generally have a minimum of 10 to 15 projects in the office at any one time, in various stages of completion.

I do use specification/tracking sheets that I have developed over time. These sheets have space for contact information and style information for each project and are kept in my master file. I would really like to spend some time investigating electronic tracking, and maybe, when I catch up, I will.

BARBARA STROUP

I index fewer books per year than I would like so I usually work on one project at a time. Here's how I keep myself on top of a typical book project: I like to have my project "diary" on my desk in hard copy, not on my computer screen.

As soon as the contract and/or page proofs arrive, I print a one-month calendar using one of the templates in Lotus Word or Microsoft Publisher. This calendar stays on a clipboard near my computer for the duration of the current project. I red pencil the start and due dates and put an X through those days that are unavailable to the project (trips to Paris, lunch at the White House). Given the number of pages and the number of days until the deadline, I calculate how many pages per day I need to finish, and I allow ample time for editing toward the end. (I also allow for all those tasks that come up at the end of a project: copying to diskette or electronic transmission, writing the cover letter, creating the invoice, and mailing tasks.)

This calculation gives me a pages-per-day figure as a goal, but the text may or may not cooperate with me. There may be days in which the subject allows me to speed up considerably and other times when I'll need to go a lot slower, especially at the beginning of a project. As I work through the chapters, I like to know how I am progressing, so each day I record what I accomplished: number of pages, chapters, etc., and what queries developed. I like to calculate what I am earning per hour; therefore, I record the time I spend on phone calls, research, and ancillary tasks associated with the project.

After the index is completed, I write the total number of hours on the same calendar page and I file it with some sample index pages and my contract(s) from that editor. It provides a quick reference for future calls from the same publisher: Did pages arrive late? Were there unanswered queries? And, for calls for work on similar subject matter, was I able to keep to my daily goal or did the density of the subject matter slow me down? Because this system helps me analyze how fast I work, I can quickly calculate the time I will need when a similar project is proposed.

I hope this system is helpful to other indexers, and I look forward to reading about tracking systems that others use.

Portions of this chapter appeared as the column "The ABCs of Project Management," in Key Words, *Vol. 5, No.6, Nov./Dec. 1997.*

Chapter 10

Tips for a Winning Proposal

Janet Perlman © 2001

You've been asked to put together a proposal for a potential client. It's a job you want, one you can do. You really want to go after it! But you've never made up a proposal before.

This is a familiar scenario for many freelancers. Let me reassure you. It's not as difficult as you think. Putting together a winning proposal is simply a question of putting together one good-looking package with all the material your client will need to go through his or her decision-making process.

If the job being offered is not a complex one, you will not have to do a lot of figuring. The cost will be fairly straightforward, as will the time element. For that type of job, I use a fairly simplified proposal and/or proposal letter, which is included at the end of this article.

But what if the project is a complex one, such as a cumulative index, a series of indexes that will be cumulated, or a set of journal issues for the year or for multiple years.

In that case, there is a bit more work to preparing the proposal. I try to limit my time to about one-half a day (this arbitrary figure is mine). It's the amount of time I'm willing to spend assuming no financial compensation. (Proposals are done at no cost to the client, in my experience!) Obviously, the bigger the job, the more time you will be willing to give to creating the proposal.

Don't worry if it takes you longer the first time. It took me a lot longer, and then I realized I had spent an entire day and worked for nothing unless, of course, I got the job. It gets easier, and you will find ways of streamlining the process.

PREPARATION

You will need to do some thinking about how you would go about the project and what the product would look like. You will need to know how much time you need and how much it will cost the client (the price). Those are things you really do in your mind with any project. They are the basic prep work of analyzing any job.

A bit of research and a nice chat with the client will stand you in good stead. Find out what you can about the client's products, who the audience for this project is, and how it fits in with the other products. A good discussion of the job with your client will give you a better feel of the client's needs.

BUILDING A PARTNERSHIP

I look upon this portion of the preparation as building a partnership with the client. It is your opportunity, through telephone conversations and, if the project is sizeable enough, an onsite meeting to hear what the client really wants and zero in on some specifics.

In some cases, when the client is unsure of what he or she wants ("We just need an index."), this is your opportunity to shine by helping the client to formulate a clearer needs statement. By doing this, you have defined the problem in terms the client is comfortable with and that are clear to you. The client will come away from this contact feeling as if you have provided a service by clarifying the job, and you have come away from it knowing just what he or she wants.

GET A SAMPLE OF THE MATERIAL

The heart of a good proposal is the cost estimate. So, when discussing the project at the outset, request a copy of the journal or book being indexed. It is impossible to make a good proposal without seeing the material you're going to work on and actually working on it.

CREATE A SAMPLE INDEX

Next, get to work creating a sample index. Use a large enough batch of pages, or a large enough portion of a journal issue, to make up an index that is a representative sample of what is in the material you will be indexing. I try to have about a four-page index (pages in MS Word, that is) when I'm done.

You may be thinking that this is a lot of extra work. It really isn't—it's worth the effort. It serves two purposes. First, it will be used to work up the cost estimate. How? By making up this sample, you will be able to estimate the length of time needed, the depth of indexing required, and the length of the index, as well as any potential problems in data entry (e.g., foreign characters, technical terms, symbols). The added benefit is that you now have a sample index to include as part of your proposal!

ESTIMATE THE COST

When I work on the sample index, I keep track of my time. I know how many pages I've done, so I now can project that figure into a time estimate, albeit a rough one, of how long the indexing and computer input will take. You could put together a cost estimate based on time alone. Don't forget to add in the time for editing on a large project. It can be considerable.

Also, from the sample index, you know how many pages you indexed. If you are working on a proposal for a journal or an oversized book, you may have to estimate how many book pages that equals so you can estimate the job cost on the basis on a per-page rate as we usually do with back-of-the-book indexes.

Finally, you can see how long the index will be, so you can provide yourself with a third cost estimate on the basis of per-entry cost.

When I go through this process, the figures usually come out fairly close to each other. Whether figured by time, by per-page rate, or per-entry rate, you can come to a good estimate.

If you are working on journals, it might pay to translate the cost figures into either a per-issue cost, or a per-article cost. This makes it finite for the client. The more insight the client has into what you did to arrive at the final cost figure, the more it will be taken seriously.

THE PROPOSAL ITSELF

Now that you have a sample index, you know how much time you will need to complete the project, and you have your cost estimate. You are ready to get into the nitty-gritty of putting the actual proposal together.

I have outlined the important elements of a Letter Proposal (more simplified) and the Narrative Proposal (more complex) on the following pages. I have also provided a sample Letter Proposal. Don't feel bound to duplicate the sample. Be creative. This is provided for instructional purposes only.

Don't forget to include the sample index and your credentials as part of your proposal!

LETTER PROPOSAL

The Letter Proposal is used for more limited, straightforward projects. This is the one I use for most of my proposals. It's shorter and requires less preparation time. Elements of the Letter Proposal are the cover letter, and a one- or at most two-page document that forms the proposal. The cover letter, which echoes the terms and information set forth in the proposal itself, is set up so that it can serve as a contract when signed by both parties. If you decide to include a Sample Index, modify the wording of the Cover Letter and of the Proposal itself to indicate that you are including the sample.

LETTER PROPOSAL—COVER LETTER

On your letterhead, of course!

February 4, 2001

James Smith
8000 South Oracle Road
Tucson, AZ 85704

Re: Index preparation for *History of Mining in Arizona*

Dear James,

Thanks to you and Mike Williams for recommending me for preparation of the cumulative index for three volumes of *History of Mining in Arizona* to appear in Volume 3, about to be published. I am pleased to provide you with this quote for your funding agency, the Mining Foundation of the Southwest.

My fee for preparation of the cumulative index for the three volumes will be $X,XXX, which will be invoiced upon completion of the work. I will submit the index as a computer file and hard copy. Let me know which of these file formats—MS Word, ASCII, or RTF—works best for you.

The final cumulative index will be ready for you by March 18, 2001. I will try to get it done earlier but cannot promise.

This letter, when signed by both parties, will serve as our agreement to these terms. To confirm your acceptance, please return one signed copy of this letter to me in the attached self-addressed stamped envelope.

Sincerely,

Janet Perlman

I accept the terms specified in this Letter of Agreement and the attached Proposal dated February 4, 2001.

Signed: _____   Date: _____

Title: _____

ACTUAL LETTER PROPOSAL

On your letterhead, of course!

PROPOSAL

PROJECT NAME: *History of Mining in Arizona* (cumulative index)

SCOPE OF WORK: Indexer will provide an alphabetical, professional quality cumulative subject index that includes Volumes I-III of the above title. Text pages and photographs will be indexed. All page references in the index will contain both volume number and page number.

TIME REQUIRED: The final index will be delivered on March 18, 2001 assuming page proofs of all volumes are received by March 1, 2001. Should page proofs of Volume III be delayed beyond March 1, 2001, this due date may also be delayed.

PRODUCT DELIVERY: Indexer will deliver cumulative indexes as an MS Word, ASCII, or RTF file, on disk, accompanied by a printout.

COST OF SERVICES: The fee for index preparation will be $X,XXX.

TERMS OF PAYMENT: Indexer will invoice upon submission of the completed cumulative index. Payment in full is due within 30 days.

Prepared February 4, 2001

ELEMENTS OF PROPOSALS

➤ THE POINT
After a word of thanks, get directly to what you have to offer, focusing on results and on the advantages of working with you.

➤ PROPOSED PROJECT
What are you planning to do for your client? Include a brief description.

➤ ANTICIPATED OUTCOMES
If you are going to make recommendations that will save your client $1 million, tell him so here. If you are going to train your client, say so. If the project is summarized in the Proposed Project section, skip this.

➤ ACTION PLAN
Outline the steps, along with any assumptions that you are making and any other details that your clients should know. This is an elaboration on the Proposed Project. This is where you say what you WILL and WILL NOT do, and what you expect the client to do to make it possible for you to do your work.

➤ PRICE
The bottom line.

➤ PAYMENT TERMS
Be specific.

➤ NEXT STEPS
Put the ball in your prospective client's court and explain what the client needs to do. The simplest way is to ask your potential client to accept your proposal by signing it at the bottom and returning the original, signed proposal to you. As soon as the client signs and returns the proposal to you, you have a contract binding on both parties.

Narrative Proposal

The Narrative Proposal is used to bid on more complex projects, perhaps those with multiple sections or requiring a team approach. Some of elements of this type of proposal are:

- Cover Letter
- Title Page
- Table of Contents
- Executive Summary
- Anticipated Outcomes
- Scope of Work
- Schedule (detailed)
- Fee
- Qualification and Experience (perhaps of the team members)
- Resume(s)
- Letters of Reference

A Narrative Proposal is a lengthier document. You might want to use tabs of colored separators between the sections. You will probably want to have the proposal bound professionally to improve its appearance.

As you can see, this type of document requires more time, effort and expense. It is only for big projects, projects worth that amount of time and effort.

For most projects, if a Letter Proposal is too simplified, a variation somewhere between the elements of the Letter Proposal and the Narrative Proposal would be appropriate. Following acceptance of the proposal, a confirming letter would be generated, and then a formal contract.

PRESENTATION HELPS!

Without being ostentatious, make your proposal look GOOD! Print it on a good business paper, perhaps a tan or cream color. Include your résumé, and that should look wonderful, too!

Even if it is small, I never fold a proposal and put it into a regular business envelope. It will never look good after being folded. Give your proposal the importance it deserves—put it in a pocket folder and mail it flat.

I usually choose a dark glossy folder, chic but businesslike. Make sure the folder is notched so that you can slip your business card into the notches on the inside left-hand side.

Put some materials in the left pocket and others on the right. Perhaps the résumé and list of projects/books completed on the left and your title page and proposal on the right. Be creative.

Most important, send it by overnight delivery, so it arrives quickly. This is money well spent even if you use the two-day rate. It looks important. It looks as if you take the proposal seriously. It won't land in a pile of mail on somebody's desk and lay there unopened.

WHAT'S NEXT?

I don't usually have face-to-face meetings with clients. Perhaps your client is in your city, and you can actually present the proposal to the client. More often than not, I send the proposal with a cover letter by overnight delivery.

GET FEEDBACK

I usually call a few days later and ask if the client received the proposal and has any questions. At that point, you may get some feedback right away, or you might be told that the proposal is under consideration.

If there is feedback, listen carefully. The client may have been surprised at the cost. It may be way too high. Or, there may be something he or she didn't tell you that should have been included. Volunteer to revise or tweak and resubmit the proposal if it is a job you want.

RESUBMIT THE PROPOSAL

It is important once again to communicate well at this point. If the money is out of the client's league, find a way to pare down the cost without compromising quality, and let the client know during the conversation that you can think of ways to save time and lower the cost. Perhaps you could omit that last level of indexing. Maybe you went further in depth than the client needed. Or perhaps a keyword index would be sufficient for that type of material, rather than an in-depth index. Let the client know that you can resubmit, and do so.

WRAPPING IT UP

Stay in touch with your client but do understand that other proposals may have been received also, so it takes time to evaluate them.

Even if you have to negotiate price one more time, you are close to ending the process. Be aware, also, that the person you are speaking to may or may not be the decision-maker, and that may make a difference in how you proceed.

ETHICS, PLEASE!

A final word on ethics. As freelancers, we have choices to make about how we do business. I hope you will choose the ethical way.

The following are some areas to be careful of:
- Conflicts of interest
- Ability to do the job (or lack thereof), i.e., qualifications
- Insider information—keep it to yourself!
- Fees and timekeeping
- Honesty

Do the right thing, and don't misrepresent yourself. Don't make claims you can't back up, and stay honest! You have a professional reputation to protect.

TIPS FOR A WINNING PROPOSAL

- Don't assume that your clients know that you can do the best job. State your qualifications.
- Provide stellar references. State your track record.
- Help your client develop the specs for the job.
- Clearly define the boundaries of the job. Say what you will and will not do.
- Be prepared to answer every question. Anticipate the questions. Know how you can lower that bid.
- Be proactive in following up.
- Leave room to negotiate—be flexible on terms.
- Be prepared with alternatives.
- Know your limits. Make sure you know your bottom price. Know how long you need to do the job. Don't let yourself be pushed.
- Don't be afraid to say NO if necessary. You will have to live with your own decision later and the contract you end up with.

ADDITIONAL RESOURCES

Thomas L. Greenbaum, *The Consultant's Manual,* John Wiley & Sons, 1990.
Bob Nelson and Peter Economy, *Consulting for Dummies,* IDG Books, 1997.

A version of this chapter, which is adapted from a workshop given at the 1998 ASI Conference in Seattle by the author and Noeline Bridge, appeared in Key Words, *Vol. 7, Issue 3, May/June 1999.*

Chapter 11

Outsourcing the Outsourcing

Enid L. Zafran © 2001

Unlike many freelance indexers who work as a solo operation, I have used subcontractors in my indexing business for over a decade. They are not employees, and that is an important distinction. For tax purposes, it means they receive a 1099 from me at the end of the year. It also means I am not responsible for withholding tax, workers' comp, or any other tax-related reporting and contributions. However, I must be careful that they qualify under the various IRS tests to keep the subcontractor status. They have their own equipment (e.g., I do not provide them with PCs or desks), they work primarily offsite (e.g., not at my home office and most likely at their own home offices), and though I provide the work with some instructions, they are not under "my control" (e.g., they can refuse the assignment unlike an employee who does whatever work is assigned).

I have tried various techniques for finding these people. I started with a core group of indexers whom I had trained during my career at different publishing companies. That gave me a great headstart. Since I had trained them, we all indexed in a similar manner so when we work on a large project, the indexing blends well together. I also knew the quality of their work, their strengths and weaknesses, and their level of commitment to meeting a deadline. The latter can sometimes be the most important trait of all, since you can usually fix up a few problems in the work, but having no work product on deadline day is the worst scenario since you can be left in the lurch.

Over a period of years, some from this initial group have stopped indexing for one reason or another, varying from family commitments to illness to the strain of combining outside work with a full-time job. So, I have had to look for new indexers. ASI local chapter meetings have provided me with some excellent recruitment opportunities. People just starting out frequently attend to learn about the profession and are eager to get some hands-on experience by taking entry-level tasks. I typically start them out with a task like inputting an index for a book on which I have been hired to produce for a new edition. In these instances, the publisher has provided me a print copy of the index to the former edition and can supply no existing electronic version. For legal material, there is often a tremendous correlation from one edition to the next, so having the base of the older edition's index input in Cindex™ (the indexing software I use) makes my work go much faster. This gives the new person a chance to use the software, and it also shows me how accurate a typist he or she is. Accuracy is a threshold issue to me; it is not something I can teach someone, so I need to see it demonstrated early in the working relationship with a new person.

I use other approaches in the first year with a new subcontractor. Although I have at times given a proofreading test, it is not as definitive as seeing actual work. The indexing part of updating an earlier edition is a good project for new indexers since it gives them a framework for structuring their indexing efforts. That may be one of the first indexing assignments I will give a new person. My business does a lot of table work since my specialty of legal indexing requires tables of cases, statutes, and rules. Tabling can involve an intense amount of keying with attention to detail. It gives me an excellent idea of how accurate a typist a person will be. While it may sound like a very mechanical type of work to produce tables, it involves understanding and applying many rules as well as manipulating the data in various software packages. This assignment will show me how agile the person will be when interacting with software. Since these are all areas of concern, it is important to see proof of concept.

When I have back-of-the-book indexing projects that involve many names, as in a history book or biography, I like to have the newer indexer input those for me before I begin indexing the book topically. That way as I proceed through the book in my indexing pass, I can check the accuracy of the entry. It saves me inputting time, and for projects in which the publisher has given me a certain index length but still insists on all the names being included, it shows me how much room I have left for the topical indexing.

Once I am comfortable with people in terms of meeting deadlines, accuracy, and software knowledge, I make a more substantial investment of my time. Typically, I ask them to index a book concurrently with me. At the same time I am indexing it, they are indexing it as well. Then we compare our indexing. This is one of the most instructive exercises I do with new indexers. I pay them for this work although at a lower rate than if I had assigned them the book on their own. This will give the new people a lot more confidence to do an index. Even if they have taken the USDA course, they find this real-life indexing work to be instructive.

Sometimes I have found experienced indexers who are looking for subcontracting assignments. Why do these indexers want to take work from another indexer? Perhaps they are not interested in finding and dealing with their own clients. Maybe they work at an in-house indexing job and want to make some money on the side but not set up a business which requires the time to seek out customers.

My experiences with these people have been varied. Although they call themselves "indexers," the amount of training and nature of their previous indexes can be deceiving. They may, in fact, have developed bad habits yet insist they are right. Sometimes they fail to follow the directions for a project and assume the style they have always used will be the proper style. Indexers who have worked internally for a publisher or worked with only one publisher think that what they learned previously will apply to all projects. It is a shock to them to learn many valid styles and guidelines can apply to indexes, and the indexer must be flexible and adapt to the client's specifications. The partial cause of this problem comes from failure to read, understand, and follow directions. When I see this problem more than once with the same person, it is unlikely I will use him or her a third time. Usually, I consider the first occurrence to be a possible miscommunication, but if it happens again (and right away on the next project), then I just don't use that person again.

Unlike overseeing employees within an organization, you are under no obligation to try to do remedial work with subcontractors. They don't get annual reviews or regular feedback on a form from a Human Resources (HR) department. They will not have a required probation and warning period. If the work shows serious problems, if they fail to meet the deadline, or if they ignore the directions more than once, then I just don't use them again.

By now you may be wondering why use other people at all since it sounds as if they may create additional headaches for you? I do it for several reasons. It allows me to take on "big" projects in my business. Not all indexers (especially solo indexers) can handle a project that will need over 100,000 entries in five months. By having multiple workers I can offer that type of service and can meet the needs of large projects. The compensation for a huge project moves beyond the usual indexing fee since the publisher knows it demands expertise, coordination, and management skills.

As long as an indexer works alone, the indexer will have total control over every aspect of the work. That is definitely a plus and can be very attractive for people. However, that indexer's income will always be limited to exactly as much work as one person can do. That may be sufficient depending upon the goals of the indexer. However, if the indexer wants to move to the next income level, a price hike of another $0.25/page will not do it.

The most significant way to step up your income is to have helpers and earn from their work. At the same time, you need to keep these people happy so they continue to take work from you, so you must pay them fairly. This has caused me at times to make very little from a job. In fact, a couple of years ago I had to do a serious analysis of my business to see why I was making so little personally when I had so much work. I was taking too many small jobs that paid in the range of $200-$400 and then farming the work out. My cut would end up being $50 or less, yet I had the administrative end of dealing with the customer and the time-consuming task of fixing up work and processing it. Since then, I refuse all work that pays less than $700 (with the exception of occasionally doing something small for a steady customer). I tell potential clients when they offer me a small job that I have a minimum of $700. For projects under 200 pages, that means they frequently take the job elsewhere. It has been a good business decision for me, and it makes it easier for me to decline less profitable jobs.

Since most of the people who work for me are moonlighting or have a working spouse, I do not pay them until I receive payment from the customer. I tell them about this arrangement up front so there is no confusion on this point. For the few whose freelance work is their sole source of revenue, I make it a priority to pay within a couple of weeks of receipt of their material. This policy of paying mostly after I receive payment has enabled me to avoid cash flow problems. However, on large jobs I have had occasionally to dip into savings in order to compensate subcontractors who could not wait the five to six weeks until I would be paid. If you decide to use subcontractors, it is important to discuss the payment arrangements early in the relationship since a misunderstanding in this area can seriously impair future relations.

I have heard other indexers who use subcontractors (or, have employees in a small indexing shop) express concern about the helpers "stealing away" their clientele. When I first moved to the DC area, I did some indexing work for EEI, a large editorial operation in Alexandria, VA. They have their employees sign a noncompetition agreement to ensure against this situation since the employee may decide to go on his or her own and underbid EEI on a future job. I have never taken this step of having subcontractors sign anything agreeing that they would not contact my clients and offer their services to them directly. At present, my philosophy is that there is enough work, and I am not nervous about this. I have a well-established reputation with my clients, and I am not their sole source of indexing nor is any one client my sole source of income. For the most part, I expect subcontractors to behave ethically and so far I have not been disappointed.

Rarely do I have the indexer deal directly with the customer. Typically, I handle all the client contact, so the subcontractor does not have direct interaction with the publisher or packager. I can answer many questions from the freelancer since I have a broader knowledge of the customer's requirements from doing many jobs over many years. When a question does need an answer from the customer, I forward it as my own and then get back to the indexer with the response. The material comes from the publisher to me and then goes from me to the freelancer. I build the cost of any extra shipping or copying into the bill I will send the customer (for example, if charging an hourly rate, I add another hour for the shipping).

The last issue that I will discuss deals with the relationship with the clients. On occasion I have had to sign agreements with publishers that either I will do all the work myself or I will give them resumés for the subcontractors for them to approve. I have found the best policy is to make clear that you do not work alone so the publishers know that the work may be done by others (although I assure them that I review it and stand behind it). If I agree to do the work personally, then I do that. But once you have an established course of dealing with publishers and they know that you will be having help with projects, that does not seem to present a problem.

For me the benefits of using subcontractors outweigh the negatives. I like to manage large projects and could not do that work without additional indexers. It adds an extra social dimension to an otherwise solo business. And the personal satisfaction that comes from running an indexing business that can handle over 120 deadlines a year makes it worthwhile.

Chapter 12

Late Payment Blues

Janet Perlman © 2001

You approach your mailbox with anticipation, anxious to see if that check you've been waiting for is there. You flip through the mail quickly. Dang! It's not there, and everyday you say, "Tomorrow I'll check on it."

If you have been indexing for any length of time, you've experienced this scenario. It's one that's equally familiar to long-time indexers and newer indexers. I could have subtitled this article "the joys of cash flow" or "life as a freelancer."

Let's take a look at some options. There are things you can do at certain points in the freelance process that are fairly effective, and some others that you can try that are not as effective but are nonetheless often tried. This discussion is a compilation of remarks from the ASI listserv (ASI-L) discussion that took place in December 1999 and January 2000.

The discussion began when somebody asked about how to handle additional work from a company that already owes you money. Willa MacAllen answered: "One of my rules of thumb when working for clients is never to let money owed get to be too large. For instance, if I'm on a project and am owed over $1,000, I'll hold off work until the client pays. I don't want the client to assume that I'll work for free. ... As freelancers, we have a right to decide how to handle situations in cases where a client is late in paying."

Others held the opinion that refusing to do any more work and saying why would be a reasonable thing to do, and that there should be no fear of antagonizing the client. This client is a problem client anyway, so to lose such a client would not be a great loss.

Who are these problem clients? Are there any signs or signals as to when or which client to beware of? Not really. Many on the listserv have told stories of major publishers or packagers who were delinquent because of financial difficulties and of a disregard for the small business or freelancer.

Julia Marshall told this story: "Last fall, I had a terrible time collecting from a major publisher who had been one of my best clients. What happened was that this publisher had been bought out and everyone on the production staff of the old company had been let go, including the production editor with whom I had worked on the project for which I needed to be paid. It was the same situation that a lot of you have described of calling and e-mailing with no response. I persisted though and called some other contacts in the company and finally got paid."

Elliot Linzer recounts: "I am still owed money from one client for work I finished many months ago. It is more common for my clients to be late than on time in their payments. Just about all book packagers tend to pay late. They practically have to. Usually, packagers will pay a freelancer only after they have been paid by their client. Often the big publishers fall behind in their invoices. Big publishers also have the problem of six employees who have to sign off before a check is issued. If one of them is on vacation, sick, or at an out-of-town business meeting, the invoice or purchase order may just sit on the desk collecting dust. Then there is the problem of the lost invoice, ..."

It isn't only American freelancers who have this difficulty. Michael Wyatt from Australia participated in the discussion and told of his difficulties in collecting from clients. He had the same problems as American freelancers did.

Ideas thrown out to ameliorate payment problems were the following: include a statement on the invoice of late fee due if payment is late, request a retainer fee from the client, discuss with the client of who owns the rights to the index in case of nonpayment, and advocate on behalf of freelancers by your professional association.

Retainer fees are an issue on which those on the listserv were divided. Some said they would request a retainer for a large project. There was recognition that it is not standard operating practice in our industry and could not be used as a matter of course. It might be a request best reserved for a major project, in which such a thing could be written into a proposal and/or contract.

There was a consensus, however, about the need to make follow-up phone calls and resubmit the bill, if necessary, when an invoice goes beyond 30 days past invoice date. Since the reason for lateness is not known, that is a logical and good place to begin making inquiries. Most freelancers will agree that they have heard just about everything in response to such inquiries. This writer herself has had an editor confess to having lost the invoice; another owned up to "finding it stuck in a pile of papers." The Accounting Department is often blamed, sometimes rightfully so. The approval process is one place where delays are introduced. Invoices have even "vanished." There is nothing else a freelancer can do at the outset except make polite inquiry. After the outset, the freelancer must often get creative.

Julia Marshall wrote: "My invoice says that I must receive payment within 30 days. If I don't receive payment, I tack on a 15 percent surcharge to the total fee. I've never collected this fee, even from the client mentioned above although I wish I had. I figure that that 15 percent surcharge pays for the time that I spend calling, e-mailing, and sending letters. I wish now that I had stuck to my guns with the above-mentioned client and said that I wanted that 15 percent fee because of all the time that I did spend trying to collect. But, by the time they were resolving the issue, I was just relieved to get paid."

This is pretty much the experience of most freelancers. Many of us have such statements on our invoices but do not have success in collecting the extra fee.

Nancy Mulvany suggests the following statement on the invoice: "Invoice is payable upon receipt, delinquent after 30 days. A late charge of x (I use 40 dollars) will be applied to past due accounts. Upon full payment of this invoice, all rights, including copyright, will be assigned to the client named above."

She points out that copyright cannot be ignored even if you do not use a formal contract, but that a formal contract clarifies and strengthens your position. Since many of us as freelancers work "on a handshake" without the benefit of a formal contract, perhaps we each need to rethink this issue for our own protection.

Nancy also had a suggestion for collecting on this penalty fee: "I collect the fee by billing separately for it. Whenever I have done this, I have been paid. I don't do this every time a client is late. I call them and figure out what is going on. The rare times that 60 days goes by, they get a Second Demand for Payment, along with the late charge. They are informed that they have to pay up within 30 days, or they will receive a Final Demand for Payment which will be due and payable within five business days. I've only had to go this far two times. In one case, they paid promptly; in the other case, I initiated small claims proceedings. In the end they settled, paid the invoice plus all of my court costs, Federal Express costs, process of service costs, etc."

Back to the discussion of who owns rights to the index. Dan Connolly wrote as follows: "In reflecting further, I wonder if we could take the opportunity to explain (in small, legalese print) why you own the copyright. It's entirely likely that your editor and the rest of the folk (outside of legal) would be surprised to hear it."

Dan continues: "I'm no lawyer so I don't recommend that anyone put this language in their invoices or anywhere else. I just think that indexers can give themselves (and their profession) a boost by making this point of fact widely known among publishers and editors."

Nancy added as follows: "I assign the rights in a contract (agreement). I have no interest in retaining rights to most of my indexes. However, I do have an interest in getting paid. So, assignment of rights can definitely be used as club."

(Disclaimer: As we discuss assignment of rights and wording in invoices and contracts, please keep in mind that this article is a recounting of discussions and should not be understood or construed as offering legal advice or instruction.)

An interesting discussion followed on what role the ASI or any other professional organization could play in this matter.

Dan Connolly wrote: "I think that the indexing organizations might want to look at taking up some sort of banner for freelance indexers. ... it might be worthwhile to actively promote the knowledge that freelance indexers own the copyright of indexes that are unbought (not paid for). Advocacy of our rights and publicity of the same do appear to benefit indexing as a field, in addition to indexers as people."

Dorothy DiRienzi offered: "I do not know anything about tax status being jeopardized, but the legal entanglements that might ensue strike me as an extraordinary commitment that probably goes way beyond the capacity of the volunteer board and extant monies to support. Moreover, I would dislike seeing litigation or whatever on behalf of individuals take over the primary functions of the societies, which I suspect might easily occur. We are a small group that is struggling for identification from publishers and editors who know less and less, I fear, about what we do. If our professional organization were to become embroiled in disputes with publishers, it would be additionally difficult for it to advocate using professional indexing services."

This writer has some limited knowledge of the issues involved in advocacy of this kind by the ASI and/or its Board. There are some good legal reasons, having to do with both the tax status as a 501(c)3 organization, as well as the issues about the possibility of restraint of trade lawsuits, that preclude the ASI from playing an active advocacy role in identifying or "blacklisting" publishers or packagers who pay slowly or don't pay.

It may be entirely appropriate, however, for ASI to obtain legal opinion and embark on an educational campaign for all, freelancers and publishers, about copyright and ownership rights vis-à-vis indexes. A clear statement of the law in such matters would be informative for all.

The listserv discussion was a lively sharing by many, and I'm sure proved informative to both novice as well as experienced indexers. It was our listserv at its best. And it served as a reminder to all that technique, method, and quality of the index notwithstanding, we are out there in the business world, and that we must be informed and act astutely as business people to ensure we are paid in a timely manner.

This chapter is reprinted from Key Words, *Vol. 8, Issue 2, March/April 2000.*

Index

A

Accounts payable, 1-2
    See also Business expenses
Accounts receivable, 2
    See also Income; Payment
Acquisitions editors' responsibilities, 25
American Society of Indexers (ASI)
    legal advocacy by, 74
    sample contract, 5
Authors, communicating with, 30

B

Book production
    assigning freelancing work, 27-28
    personnel involved, 25-26
    schedules and, 26-27
    timelines, 29
Book publishers' rates, 45-46
Brochures, for indexers, 9
Budgeting, for indexers, 1
Bundled jobs, 45
Business correspondence, 19-20
Business expansion, 6-10
    financial aspects of, 7-8
    incorporating, 8
    marketing for, 8-9
    outsourcing, 7-8, 67-70
    quality control and, 10
    scheduling and, 9
    subcontracting, 7-8
    time management and, 10
Business expenses, 2, 21-22
    equipment, 3-4, 14
    home office deduction, 3, 22
    mail and delivery services, 19-20, 38
    software, 4, 14
Business hours, moonlighting indexer, 18
Business letterhead, 20
Business management
    contracts, 5, 29
    independent contractor status, 31-36
    late fees, 72-73
    late payment, 71-74
    letter of agreement, 29
    payment. *See* Payment
    project management, 53-55
    proposal writing, 57-65
    retainer fees, 72
    setting fees. *See* Setting fees
    time management, 6, 10, 16, 20-21
Business phone, 18

C

Cellular phone, 18
Charging by the entry, 43-44
Clendenen, Joanne, 47
Clients
    contracts with, 5, 29
    communicating with, 18-20
    relationships with, 5
Communicating with author, 30
Communicating with clients, 18-20
Computer equipment, 51
Computer software. *See* Software
Conflict of interest, moonlighting indexers, 17

Connolly, Dan, 73
Contracts, with client, 5, 29
Copyright of indexes, 29, 73-74
Corporation, forming, 8
Correspondence, with clients, 19-20

D

Delivery services
    for proposal, 59, 63-64
    use of, 19-20, 38
DiRienzi, Dorothy, 73-74
DOL (U.S. Department of Labor) and freelance status, 31

E

Editorial managers' responsibilities, 26
Editors
    relationships with, 5
    responsibilities of, 25
EIN (Employer Identification Number), 40
Electronic files, rates for indexing of, 38-39
E-mail, moonlighting indexer and, 19
Embedded indexing, setting fees for, 38-39
Employees, tax implications of having, 7
Employer Identification Number (EIN), 40
Employers of moonlighting indexers, 14-15, 17, 22-23
Employment law, independent contractor status, 31-36
Equipment, for working indexers, 3-4, 14
Ergonomics, 50-51
Estimated taxes, 4
Ethics
    moonlighting, 17
    proposal writing, 65
    subcontractors, 70
Executive editors' responsibilities, 25
Expenses. *See* Business expenses
Express mail, 19-20, 38

F

Fax machine, 4, 19
Feedback from clients, 30
Fees. *See* Setting fees
FICA, 2
Finances, 1

accounts payable, 1-2
accounts receivable, 2
business expansion and, 7-8
invoices, 2, 30, 40, 72
moonlighting indexer, 21-22
recordkeeping, 2, 21
software for, 5
Formatting the index, 29-30
Freelancing
    benefits of, 10-11
    contracts, 5, 29
    equipment needed by, 3-4, 14
    estimating a job, 58-59
    expanding your business, 6-10, 67-70
    finances, 1-2
    independent contractor status, 31-36
    marketing, 4-5
    moonlighting, 13-24
    office space for, 47-51
    outsourcing by, 7-8, 67-70
    payment, 2, 29, 40, 69-74
    project management for, 53-55
    scheduling by, 6, 9, 15, 20-21, 27, 53-55
    setting fees by, 37-41
    software used by, 4, 14
    subcontracting by, 7-8, 67-70
    supplies used by, 3-4
    taxes and, 2-3, 14, 21-22, 67
    time management for, 6, 10, 16, 20-21
Furniture, office, 47-51

H

Home office deduction, 3, 22
Hourly rates, 36, 38-40

I

Income
    See also Payment
    record of, 2
    setting level of, 7
Incorporating, 8
Independent contractor status, 31-36

Indexers
client's request for proof of, 31
criteria for, 32-33
protecting the worker with, 34-35
subcontractor, 67
equipment needed by, 3-4, 14
feedback from client, 30
freelancers. *See* Freelancing
moonlighting, 13-24
project management by, 53, 55
refusing work, 9, 45
saving page proofs, 30, 51
scheduling work, 6, 9, 15, 20-21, 27
software used by, 4, 14
time management by, 6, 10, 16, 20-21

Indexes
archiving, 51
copyright of, 29, 73-74
formatting, 29-30
quality of, 5, 10

Indexing software, 14

Indexing work
assigning, 27
bundled jobs, 45
client feedback, 30
communicating with author, 30
embedded indexing, 38-40
nonpayment for, 29
outsourcing, 7-8, 67-70
payment for. *See* Payment
refusing, 9, 45
sample index, approval of, 30
scheduling of, 6, 9, 15, 20-21, 27
setting fees, 37-41, 45-46, 69, 70
tracking sheets, 53-55

Internal Revenue Service (IRS)
estimated taxes, 3
independent contractor status, 31-36, 67
1099 form, 7-8, 67

Invoices
contents of, 2, 30, 40
copies of, 2
payment terms, 40, 72

L

Late fees, 72-73
Late payment, 71-74
Leach, Anne, 53-54
Legal advocacy, by ASI, 74
Letter of agreement, 29
Letter Proposal, 59-61
Letterhead, 20
Lighting, indexer's office, 47, 50
Linzer, Elliot, 72
Low-paying clients, educating, 45-46

M

MacAllen, Willa, 71
Mailing expense, 19-20
Marketing, 4-5, 8-9, 28-29
Marshall, Julia, 71, 72
Microsoft Corp., *Vizcaino* case, 35
Moonlighting
advantages of, 15
as business, not hobby, 14-15
career path for, 16
communicating with clients, 18-20
conflict of interest for, 17
defined, 13-14
disadvantages of, 15-16
employers of moonlighters, 14-15, 17, 22-23
ethical issues for, 17
finances and, 21-22
moving to full-time, 23
reasons for, 15-16
setting priorities in, 14
taxes and, 14
ten commandments of, 24
time management, 16, 20-21
Mulvany, Nancy, 72-73

N

Narrative proposal, 63
Natural keyboard, 51
Negotiation of a proposal, 64
See also Setting fees
Newsletters, for indexers, 9

Nickerson, Alexandra, 48
Nonpayment, 29

O

Office space, 47-51
Office supplies, 3-4
Online indexing, setting fees for, 38-39
Outsourcing, 7-8, 67-70
    advantages of, 69, 70
    finding indexers, 67-68
    subcontractor as independent contractor, 67

P

Packagers, 25
Page proof, keeping, 30, 51
Payment, 2
    late fees, 72-73
    late payment, 71-74
    nonpayment, 29
    retainer fees, 72
    subcontractors, 69-70
    terms, 40, 72
    timely, 40
PDF files, 39
Per-entry rate, 43-44
Per-hour rates, 36, 38-40
Per-page rates, 37-38
Photocopiers, use of employers', 19
Production editors, 26, 27
Production managers, 26
Project editors, 26, 28, 29
Project management, 53-55
Proposals, 57-65
    contents and format of, 59-63
    estimating the cost, 58-59
    ethical considerations, 65
    letter proposal, 59-61
    narrative proposal, 63
    negotiation, 64
    opportunity to build partnership with client, 58
    preparation for writing, 57-58
    presentation, 63-64
    sample index, 48
    sending, 59, 63-64

Q

Quality control, 5, 10
Quarterly taxes, 3

R

Rates. *See* Setting fees
Receipts, 1
Receivables. *See* Payment
Recordkeeping, 41
Refusing work, 9, 45
Retainer fees, 72
Right-to-control test, 32-35
Rowland, Marilyn, 49

S

Sample indexes
    approval by authors, 30
    proposals including, 48
Scheduling, 6, 9
    See also Time management
    importance of, 27
    indexers' systems for, 53-55
    moonlighting indexers, 15, 20-21
Schroeder, Sandi, 54-55
Self-employed person, taxes for, 2-3, 7-8, 14, 21-22, 67
Self-employment tax, 3
Self-incorporation, 8
Setting fees, 37-41
    charging by the entry, 43-44
    combination rates, 40
    embedded indexing, 38-39
    estimating a job, 58-59
    hourly rates, 36, 38-40
    lowest acceptable rate, 41
    low-paying clients, 45-46
    online indexing, 38-39
    per-page rates, 37-38
    small presses, 38
    tracking sheets, 53-55
    using subcontractors, 69, 70
Shrout, Richard, 49-51
Small presses' rates, 38
Social Security taxes, 2

Software
> financial software, 4
> indexing software, 14

Stationery, 20

Stroup, Barbara, 55

Student interns, use as subcontractors, 7, 8

Subcontracting, 67-70
> ethics of subcontractors, 70
> financial aspects of, 7-8
> independent contractor status, 67
> 1099 form, 7-8, 67

Supplies, 3-4

T

Taxes, 2-3
> business expenses, 2, 21-22
> estimated taxes, 3
> funds for, 3
> home office deduction, 3, 22
> moonlighting indexers and, 14
> quarterly taxes, 3
> self-employment tax, 3
> 1099 form, 7-8, 67

Tax preparation software, 4

Telephone
> follow-up marketing calls, 28
> use by moonlighting indexer, 18

1099 form, 7-8, 67

"Tickler file," 6

Time management, 6
> business expansion and, 10
> moonlighting indexers, 16, 20-21

Tracking sheets, 53-55

U-V

U.S. Department of Labor (DOL) and
> independent contractors, 31-36

Vizcaino vs. Microsoft Corp., 35

W

Web sites, for indexers, 9

Work-for-hire clauses, 29

Work space. *See* Office space

Written agreements, 5

Wyatt, Michael, 72

More Great Books from Information Today, Inc.

Beyond Book Indexing
How to Get Started in Web Indexing, Embedded Indexing, and Other Computer-Based Media
Edited by Marilyn Rowland and Diane Brenner

Are you curious about new indexing technologies? Would you like to develop and create innovative indexes that provide access to online resources, multimedia, or online help? Do you want to learn new skills and expand your marketing possibilities? In *Beyond Book Indexing*, 12 chapters written by 10 noted indexing professionals provide an in-depth look at current and emerging computer-based technologies, and offer suggestions for obtaining work in these fields. Extensive references and a glossary round out this informative and exciting new book.

Softbound • ISBN 1-57387-081-1
ASI Members $25.00 • Non-Members $31.25

Starting an Indexing Business, 3rd Edition
Edited by Enid L. Zafran

This popular work offers advice to those entering the field of indexing. It covers indexing as a second job, as an "at home" business for a parent with young children, and as a full-time career. Starting with an introduction by Carolyn McGovern, former ASI president, who explains what an indexer is and what an indexer does, it includes articles from a range of contributors on what publishers expect, what you need to set up shop, and how to find clients. Also included are a recent ASI fee survey of members, and a sample agreement form for indexers to use when contracting for their services.

Softbound • ISBN 1-57387-074-9
ASI Members $25 • Non-Members $30

Directory of Indexing and Abstracting Courses and Seminars
Edited by Maryann Corbett

No matter what you want to learn about abstracting or indexing, this guide will help you find out where to learn it. Library professionals, online information designers, abstractor and indexer freelancers, and publishers' staffs can all find courses that suit their needs in the Directory. Included are courses from public, private, and proprietary institutions in the U.S. and Canada.

Softbound • ISBN 1-57387-056-0

ASI Members $12 • Non-Members $18

Marketing Your Indexing Services, 2nd Edition
Edited by Anne Leach

This is a collection of articles from ASI's *Key Words*, with additional chapters by Anne Leach. It includes strategies for beginning indexers and new business owners, as well as established professionals. An excellent addition to any freelancer's library.

Softbound • ISBN 1-57387-054-4

ASI Members $15 • Non-Members $20

A Glossary
Hans H. Wellisch

Includes terms used in writings on abstracting, indexing, classification, and thesaurus construction, as well as terms for the most common types of documents and their parts.

Softbound • ISBN 0-936547-35-9

ASI Members $10 • Non-Members $16

To order directly from the publisher, include $3.95 postage and handling for the first book ordered and $1.00 for each additional book. Catalogs also available upon request. Order online at www.infotoday.com and specify that you are an ASI member when ordering.

Information Today, Inc.
143 Old Marlton Pike, Medford, NJ 08055
(800)300-9868   (609)654-6266   custserv@infotoday.com